I0820552

ANCIENT WISDOM FOR MODERN READERS

■ ■ ■ ■

For a full list of titles in the series, go to https://press.princeton.edu/series/ancient-wisdom-for-modern-readers.

How to Find Happiness: An Ancient Guide to the Good Life by Marcus Tullius Cicero

How to Be Grateful: An Aztec Guide to the Art of Gratitude by Pablo of Texcoco

How to Cope: An Ancient Guide to Enduring Hardship by Boethius

How to Feel: An Ancient Guide to Minding Our Emotions by the Buddha

How to Be Caring: An Ancient Guide to a Compassionate Life by Shantideva

How to Make a Home: An Ancient Guide to Style and Comfort by Vitruvius and Guests

How to Have Willpower: An Ancient Guide to Not Giving In by Plutarch and Prudentius

How to Talk about Love: An Ancient Guide for Modern Lovers by Plato

How to Eat: An Ancient Guide for Healthy Living by a Buffet of Ancient Authors

How to Lose Yourself: An Ancient Guide to Letting Go by the Buddha and His Followers

How to Be Queer: An Ancient Guide to Sexuality by Sappho, Plato, and Other Lovers

How to Get Over a Breakup: An Ancient Guide to Moving On by Ovid

HOW TO FIND HAPPINESS

■ ■ ■ ■ ■

An Ancient Guide to the Good Life

Marcus Tullius Cicero

Selected, translated, and introduced by Katharina Volk

PRINCETON UNIVERSITY PRESS
PRINCETON & OXFORD

Published by Princeton University Press
41 William Street, Princeton, New Jersey 08540
99 Banbury Road, Oxford OX2 6JX

press.princeton.edu

GPSR Authorized Representative:
Easy Access System Europe - Mustamäe tee 50, 10621 Tallinn, Estonia, gpsr.requests@easproject.com

ISBN 9780691263397
ISBN (e-book) 9780691263403

Library of Congress Control Number 2025942796

British Library Cataloging-in-Publication Data is available

Editorial: Rob Tempio and Chloe Coy
Production Editorial: Ali Parrington
Text and Jacket Design: Heather Hansen
Production: Erin Suydam
Publicity: William Pagdatoon and Charlotte Coyne
Copyeditor: Jennifer Harris

Jacket image: GFC Collection / Alamy Stock Photo

This book has been composed in Stempel Garamond with Futura

Printed in the United States of America

1 3 5 7 9 10 8 6 4 2

CONTENTS

INTRODUCTION

Of course, we all want to be happy. *Beati certe omnes esse uolumus.*

This statement is as true today as it was when it was penned by the Roman statesman and orator Marcus Tullius Cicero, probably in early 46 BCE. But while people in modern societies turn to religion, go to therapy, read self-help books, and surf the internet for guidance, ancient Greeks and Romans seriously on the quest for happiness more often than not took recourse to philosophy. As it happens, Cicero's observation occurs in a dialogue called *Hortensius*, a work that today unfortunately survives only in fragments, but that was originally written as a so-called protreptic, a text meant to serve as a

kind of pep talk and to inspire its readers to study philosophy.

In the wake of Socrates, all ancient philosophical schools promoted paths to what the Greeks called *eudaimonia* (blessedness) and the Romans *vita beata* (the blessed life) or simply *bene vivere* (living well). It makes sense to translate these terms as "happiness," even though what the ancient thinkers envisaged was rather more than a momentary experience of elation or contentment. True *eudaimonia*, sometimes glossed as "flourishing," consisted in a continuous, holistic state of well-being, predicated on living well—that is, consistently and consciously acting in a manner understood as appropriate for human beings. Fundamentally optimistic, philosophers held that humans, as rational agents, had the capacity to reach *eudaimonia*, and typically suggested that there was just one

thing, the *summum bonum* or "greatest good," that provided the key to the good life. If you managed to secure the *summum bonum*, you had achieved happiness.

This is where things get complicated: different philosophical schools had vastly different ideas of what the *summum bonum* might be and competed with each other in what quickly became a kind of philosophical marketplace. By the time Cicero started writing philosophy in mid-first-century Rome, the two most popular schools were Epicureanism and Stoicism, whose views of the greatest good could not be more different. Epicureans believed that pleasure is what we should all strive for, while Stoics held that the path to happiness consists in virtue or moral goodness. More than two thousand years after Cicero, these philosophies are again going strong today: as numerous popular books and a

plethora of web-based resources attest, there is a significant movement of contemporary Stoicism; Epicureanism, though not quite as popular, has a fair share of self-declared modern followers as well. (How close or not these latter-day philosophical trends are to the ancient philosophical systems to which they claim allegiance is another question.)

In a way, Cicero's Roman contemporaries found themselves in a situation not unlike modern readers: they were, as we all are, looking for happiness, and may additionally have been Stoicism- or Epicureanism-curious—or simply intrigued by the promise philosophy held out of a sure path to *eudaimonia*. While philosophy was considered a Greek invention, and the dominant philosophical schools had been founded in fourth-century Athens, the Romans had long been in the habit of importing and adapting

Greek culture, and by the first century there was a positive enthusiasm for philosophy. More and more upper-class Romans read Greek philosophical books or even went to study in Greece, and increasingly, some of them openly identified as Stoics, Epicureans, or adherents of other schools.

What Rome largely lacked at this point, however, was philosophical writing of its own. There were a few Latin Epicurean treatises, and in the mid-50s, the poet Lucretius wrote *On the Nature of Things* (*De rerum natura*), a didactic poem about Epicurean natural philosophy and one of the great masterpieces of Latin literature. Other than that, however, all philosophical texts available were written in Greek.

This is where Cicero comes in. Born in 106 BCE in the town of Arpinum, Cicero had been an outsider to the governing classes at Rome

but, by sheer talent and persistence, had quickly made a name for himself as an orator and had risen through all political offices, culminating in his consulship in 63. Unfortunately, however, the mid-first century was a period of intense turmoil at Rome: this was the time when the old Republican system (largely an oligarchy with some democratic elements) was crumbling, and various individual actors were trying to concentrate power into their own hands. This led to a series of civil wars, and finally to the rise of Julius Caesar, who, after defeating the Republican forces under Pompey in the early 40s, became de facto sole ruler at Rome until his assassination in 44. Caesar's death led to another decade and a half of civil strife, until his adopted son and heir Octavian was able to defeat his opponents and establish a lasting monarchy, going down in history as the emperor Augustus.

In these developments, Cicero was on the losing side. A lifelong believer in the traditional Republic, where policy was made by the senate and where individual magistrates received executive power for no longer than a year, he opposed Caesar in the civil war and, after his party's defeat, was lucky to receive the winner's pardon. Even so, Cicero was politically powerless during Caesar's rule and deeply depressed by the state of affairs. After the assassination, he attempted to help steer Rome back to a functioning Republic, but fell victim to the shifting political alliances of this latest installment of civil war. When in 43, Octavian entered into a pact with his former foes Mark Antony and Marcus Aemilius Lepidus, the three men drew up a list of political enemies to be eliminated, Cicero among them. By the end of the year, the former consul had been brutally murdered.

Cicero was well trained in philosophy, having studied with teachers from various schools and numbering many Greek philosophers among his friends. Already in the 50s, he had written *On the Commonwealth* (*De re publica*), a dialogue on political philosophy in imitation of, but ultimately very different from, Plato's *Republic.* In the following decade, when he found himself politically sidelined and mentally restless under Caesar's rule, as well as deeply depressed by the death of his beloved daughter Tullia, Cicero decided on a more ambitious project: he would write a series of books, a kind of comprehensive course of philosophy, offering to his fellow Romans for the first time a corpus of philosophical writing in Latin. From 46 to 44, he was hard at work, penning a dozen treatises on epistemology, ethics, natural philosophy, and religion; the project came to an end when after Caesar's death, Cicero was drawn back into politics.

One of the earliest of these works is *On the Greatest Good and Evil* (*De finibus bonorum et malorum*), which provides an introduction to ethics and to the dominant philosophical schools, using the criterion of the greatest good, that hallmark of ancient ethics. (As one can see from the title, the greatest good has a counterpart in the greatest evil: if there is one thing that we must single-mindedly pursue in order to find happiness, there is also one opposite thing that we should avoid.) The work falls into five books, which recount three different dialogues, in all of which Cicero himself features as an interlocutor. The first (Books 1 and 2) discusses Epicureanism and its view of the greatest good; the second (Books 3 and 4) covers Stoicism; and the third (Book 5) considers the so-called Old Academy of Antiochus. The last was a recent and popular offshoot of Academic (Platonic) philosophy, one that also incorporated Peripatetic

(Aristotelian) and Stoic elements. Because Antiochus's doctrine does not have much name recognition today, and because many of the arguments in Book 5 return to issues already treated in Books 3 and 4, I have not included any parts of it in my selection.

The dialogue structure of *On the Greatest Good and Evil* is key: Cicero does not present the teachings of the three schools neutrally and in textbook fashion, but instead uses the conversational frame to submit each of them to interrogation and criticism. All three dialogues follow the same format: first an adherent of the philosophy in question presents its doctrine and understanding of the greatest good; then Cicero begins to point out weaknesses in his interlocutor's argument and ends up casting serious doubts on the viability of the school's ethical system. In the end, none of the three philoso-

phies is espoused, and the work ends at an impasse.

This approach is characteristic of Cicero's own philosophical stance: he was not himself an Epicurean, Stoic, or Antiochean, but instead claimed allegiance to the New or Skeptical Academy. This had been the dominant form of Academic philosophy since the third century, when thinkers in the school originally founded by Plato proposed returning to the critical mode pioneered by Plato's teacher Socrates. Rather than accepting any dogma, Academic Skeptics questioned each and every proposition, invariably concluding that firm knowledge was impossible and that the appropriate reaction was simply to withhold judgment. To be able to show the weakness of each philosophical position, the Skeptics were skilled debaters, accustomed to consider the pros and cons of every matter, a

procedure known in Latin as *in utramque partem disputare* "arguing both sides." This is exactly what Cicero does in *On the Greatest Good and Evil*, except that, rather than speaking for both sides himself, he leaves the "pro" to an interlocutor but takes on the "con" himself.

A radical Skeptic accepts no truth and will have to decide what this means for living in the real world, where, after all, informed decisions have to be made all the time. Cicero was a more moderate Skeptic, believing, as did some other followers of the New Academy, that while we cannot know the truth, we may be able to figure out what is "similar to the truth" (*verisimile*) or "probable" (*probabile*, literally "approvable"). Rather than on knowledge, we can build our day-to-day life on opinions, ad hoc approvals of what seems more likely than not. Ever on the critical alert, a Skeptic of course reserves the

right to review and revise such opinions at any moment.

In keeping with Cicero's probabilistic attitude, *On the Greatest Good and Evil* does not choose any one philosophy as correct, but it still presents certain views as being more plausible than others. There is a progression in the book, a minor plot, which gets us closer to Cicero's ideas about the path to happiness, but which still does not point us to one particular school. Readers may follow Cicero along on his quest for what is similar to the truth, or they may abandon his gentle guidance and arrive at choices all of their own.

The author is clearly not sympathetic to Epicureanism, though he does give the school a fair shot in Book 1. There, Cicero's interlocutor is the simpatico Lucius Manlius Torquatus, a young man eager to convert Cicero to the creed

of Epicurus, who gives a clear and enthusiastic account of the school's hedonism. Torquatus states straight away that the Epicurean *summum bonum* is pleasure, something that he regards as self-evident and that is also confirmed by the behavior of infants and animals, who instinctively pursue whatever is pleasurable.

Epicurean pleasure, however, is more complicated. First, it turns out that the greatest pleasure is in fact freedom from pain (pain, unsurprisingly, being the greatest evil), which crucially includes the absence of mental pains such as fear and anxiety. Second, in pursuing pleasure the Epicurean must make use of a careful calculus, sometimes forgoing immediate pleasure to avoid greater pain down the line, or even agreeing to momentary pain to secure greater pleasure in the future. In their single-minded, rational quest for pleasure, Epicureans make use of the traditional

virtues (prudence, temperance, courage, and justice), but Torquatus stresses that these virtues are used only instrumentally and not chosen for their own sakes. Similarly, friendship is considered an excellent means of achieving pleasure, even if, as Torquatus admits, this raises questions about to which extent we are supposed to feel genuine affection for our friends.

According to Torquatus, the happy person looks like this:

> Let's picture someone who in mind and body is enjoying a great many uninterrupted pleasures without any pain either present or on the horizon. What state could we call preferable to this or more desirable? For by necessity a person in this condition is also firm of spirit and fears neither pain nor death: death, because it lacks sense perception; pain,

> because if it lasts for a long time, it is typically light, and if it is severe, it tends to be short (so short duration is the upside of severity, lightness the upside of long duration). And if, in addition, the person neither shudders at the thought of the divine nor allows past pleasures to evaporate, but instead keeps rejoicing in their memory, what else could be added to this to make their condition even better? (1.40–41)

Surely, Cicero must agree.

But of course, Cicero does not agree at all. In Book 2, he homes in on the very definition of pleasure, pointing out that the Epicurean inclusion of freedom from pain under this heading flies in the face of everyday language use: no normal person, when speaking of pleasure, is referring to the simple absence of pain. The Epi-

curean conflation of painlessness and pleasure is thus at best a conceptual muddle and at worst a bait and switch. In Cicero's opinion, the Epicureans are hard-pressed to show that the pursuit of pleasure alone provides an impetus for action (even those infants and animals are not as hedonistic as they appear), and at any rate, pleasure is such a disreputable concept that it can't qualify as the *summum bonum*. Instead, virtue or moral excellence, rather than being merely instrumental for the pursuit of the greatest good, must be at least part of the greatest good itself. It remains open, however, whether virtue alone is sufficient for happiness, or whether we also need other things.

This last question is central to the following three books, beginning with the discussion of Stoicism (Books 3 and 4), a school that holds that virtue is indeed the only good. Cicero's

interlocutor in this discussion could not be more different from the amiable Torquatus: Marcus Porcius Cato the Younger was an arch-conservative Roman politician, who unlike Cicero had continued to fight Caesar in the civil war and, after his final defeat, had committed a philosophically inspired suicide. In the dialogue, Cicero depicts him as gruff and pedantic. In Cicero's description, Stoicism is much more complicated than Epicureanism, and has a lot of specialized vocabulary. When Cato keeps pointing out his Latin word choices for translating Greek Stoic technical terms, Cicero is characterizing him as a bit of a stickler—but he is also drawing attention to his own mastery in writing Latin philosophy, since those innovations in vocabulary are, after all, Cicero's own.

Cato's explanation of the Stoic *summum bonum* in Book 3 is somewhat roundabout. He

too begins with the behavior of infants, tracing the development of human nature from birth until the perfection of reason. From the very beginning, we all love ourselves and aim at self-preservation, which ultimately leads us to pursue the "first things according to nature" (*prima naturalia*). These are things that are naturally conducive to our well-being, such as health, bodily strength, and unimpaired senses; depending on the definition, certain external goods, such as wealth or a good reputation, may be worth pursuing as well.

So far, so good. The crucial step occurs when we realize that these valuable things worthy of pursuit are not in themselves "goods," but that the only good is the fully wise, fully knowledgeable, fully honorable pursuit of them. This is what virtue consists in, the *summum bonum* we all need to achieve. Apart from virtue (and vice,

the greatest evil) all things are "indifferent"; some of those indifferents are "preferred," that is, worth pursuing, while others are "dispreferred" and thus to be avoided.

By locating the good in the mindset of agents rather than in the objects of their pursuit, Stoicism succeeds in making our happiness entirely up to us and independent from any external factors. Cato demonstrates this with the image of a person who is aiming a spear at a target and whose athletic excellence consists in throwing the spear well. Whether the spear hits the target is another matter entirely: if unforeseen circumstances should prevent this desired outcome, this would in no way detract from the spear thrower's skill. Similarly, if a Stoic's virtue fails to reach its objective, this will not diminish that person's happiness. In fact, as Cato points out, the wise and virtuous Stoic will be happy even when tor-

tured. "No one is happy except the good person, and all good people are happy" (3.76).

Cicero grants the point, but does not consider it original. In Book 4, he accuses Zeno, the founder of the Stoic school, of simply having dressed up earlier philosophy, notably Peripatetic doctrine, with fancy new terminology. Other philosophers, too, believe that virtue is paramount and that we should use it to pursue valuable things like health, physical safety, wealth, and success. The only difference is that they call those objects of pursuit "goods," while the Stoics insist on their rebarbative term "preferred indifferents."

In light of the great value the Stoics place on our natural appreciation of the first things according to nature and their desirability, it is very strange, says Cicero, how they subsequently demote them by claiming that their acquisition

in fact makes no difference to us. And while the Stoics admit that human beings consist of both body and mind, their greatest good takes no account of our physical nature and is solely focused on our mental state. Cicero, by contrast, maintains that something worthy of pursuit is by definition a "good," and that while virtue is indeed the most important such thing and sufficient for happiness, the presence of other goods must surely add something to one's well-being. Would the wise and virtuous person not be even happier if *not* being tortured?

This question returns in Book 5, where Marcus Pupius Piso speaks in favor of the school of Antiochus. Piso's view resembles the one put forth by Cicero in his dialogue with Cato: virtue is by far the most valuable thing, but for the greatest happiness, we also need some additional bodily and external goods. But if we now expect

that Cicero will be happy to accede to this doctrine, we are in for a surprise: ever the Skeptic, he proceeds to shoot holes into Piso's argument, defending in turn the Stoic view. If there are goods in addition to virtue, there must also be evils other than vice, including illness, disability, poverty, and failure. Because these additional goods and evils are not in our control, neither is our happiness. We can control our virtue, and thus secure a good amount of *eudaimonia*; depending on the circumstances, however, complete happiness may not be possible for us. As soon as the good life depends on multiple factors, it threatens to elude our grasp.

The dialogue in Book 5 involves a larger audience, including Cicero's brother, his young cousin, and his friend Atticus. In the end, the brother and the cousin are leaning toward Piso's Antiochean view; Cicero stands by his Stoically

inflected criticism; and Atticus, an Epicurean, still hints at his own school's superiority. All participants, however, have enjoyed the conversation and are delighted that philosophical ideas can be expressed so well in Latin.

With these reactions, Cicero models the responses of his readers. It is up to us to approve or disapprove of any of the ideas mooted in the five books of *On the Greatest Good and Evil*, or indeed, if we have a skeptical bent, to withhold judgment. What we should do, however, is philosophize. Only in this way can we find happiness.

Further Reading

Still the best biography of Cicero is Elizabeth Rawson, *Cicero: A Portrait* (Allen Lane, 1975, much reprinted).

A perceptive overview of Cicero's philosophy can be found in Raphael Woolf, *Cicero: The Philosophy of a Roman Sceptic* (Routledge, 2015).

Julia Annas and Raphael Woolf, *Cicero: On Moral Ends* (Cambridge University Press, 2001) is an excellent translation of the entirety of *De finibus bonorum et malorum*, with helpful notes.

R. W. Sharples, *Stoics, Epicureans and Sceptics: An Introduction to Hellenistic Philosophy* (Routledge, 1996), and John Sellars, *Hellenistic Philosophy* (Oxford University Press, 2018), provide useful introductions to the philosophical schools Cicero discusses.

For Epicureanism, see further Tim O'Keefe, *Epicureanism* (University of California Press, 2009); for Stoicism, John Sellars, *Stoicism* (University of California Press, 2006).

HOW TO FIND HAPPINESS

DE FINIBUS BONORUM ET MALORUM

ON THE GREATEST GOOD AND EVIL

[12] Nos autem hanc omnem quaestionem de finibus bonorum et malorum fere a nobis explicatam esse his litteris arbitramur, in quibus, quantum potuimus, non modo quid nobis probaretur sed etiam quid a singulis philosophiae disciplinis diceretur, persecuti sumus. [13] Ut autem a facillimis ordiamur, prima veniat in medium Epicuri ratio, quae plerisque notissima est.

(. . .)

[29] Primum igitur, inquit, sic agam ut ipsi auctori huius disciplinae placet: constituam quid et quale

BOOK 1

The Allure of Epicureanism

Cicero introduces the topic of his book.

[12] I think I've laid out that whole issue of the greatest good and evil pretty thoroughly in this book, where I've tried to focus not just on what seems plausible to me, but also on the doctrines of the individual philosophical systems. [13] And to begin with what is easiest, let's have the Epicurean school up first, since a lot of people know it very well.

In a conversation with Cicero and Triarius, Torquatus explains the Epicurean view.[1]

[29] First of all, he said, I'll approach the topic in the manner approved by the founder of our

sit id de quo quaerimus, non quo ignorare vos arbitrer, sed ut ratione et via procedat oratio. Quaerimus igitur quid sit extremum et ultimum bonorum, quod omnium philosophorum sententia tale debet esse, ut ad id omnia referri oporteat, ipsum autem nusquam. Hoc Epicurus in voluptate ponit, quod summum bonum esse vult, summumque malum dolorem, idque instituit docere sic:

[30] omne animal, simul atque natum sit, voluptatem appetere eaque gaudere ut summo bono, dolorem aspernari ut summum malum et, quantum possit, a se repellere, idque facere nondum depravatum ipsa natura incorrupte atque integre iudicante. Itaque negat opus esse ratione neque disputatione quam ob rem voluptas expetenda, fugiendus dolor sit: sentiri haec putat, ut calere

school: I'll define the object of our inquiry, exactly what kind of thing it is—not because I think you don't know, but so that my speech can proceed in a rational and methodical fashion. So, we're trying to discover what the last and final good is, the one that all philosophers think has to be the goal of everything else, while itself it has no goal of its own. Epicurus says that this is pleasure; according to him, this is the greatest good, while the greatest evil is pain. And this is how he makes his case:

[30] as soon as it is born, every animal pursues pleasure and rejoices in it as in the greatest good, and it avoids pain as the greatest evil and pushes it away from itself as much as it can. And it does so when it is as yet unspoiled, with its natural judgment uncorrupted and unimpaired. Epicurus says that there is no need for reasoning or argument why pleasure should be sought and pain

ignem, nivem esse albam, dulce mel, quorum nihil oportere exquisitis rationibus confirmare, tantum satis esse admonere. Interesse enim inter argumentum conclusionemque rationis et inter mediocrem animadversionem atque admonitionem: altera occulta quaedam et quasi involuta aperiri, altera prompta et aperta indicari. Etenim quoniam detractis de homine sensibus reliqui nihil est, necesse est quid aut ad naturam aut contra sit a natura ipsa iudicari. Ea quid percipit aut quid iudicat, quo aut petat aut fugiat aliquid, praeter voluptatem et dolorem?

[31] Sunt autem quidam e nostris qui haec subtilius velint tradere et negent satis esse quid bonum

avoided: it's something we perceive with our senses, just as we perceive that fire is hot, snow white, and honey sweet. None of these things needs to be shored up with clever reasoning, you only need to point them out. For there is, according to Epicurus, a difference between rational arguments and syllogisms on the one hand and everyday observations and experiences on the other. The former disclose things that are abstruse and hidden, as it were, while the latter point out matters that are out in the open and obvious. And since there is nothing left when you take away someone's sense perception, it is nature itself that must decide what is either according or contrary to nature. And what criterion does nature perceive and use to judge what to pursue and what to avoid, other than pleasure and pain?

[31] But there are some Epicureans who prefer to make this point in a more sophisticated

sit aut quid malum sensu iudicari, sed animo etiam ac ratione intellegi posse et voluptatem ipsam per se esse expetendam et dolorem ipsum per se esse fugiendum. Itaque aiunt hanc quasi naturalem atque insitam in animis nostris inesse notionem, ut alterum esse appetendum, alterum aspernandum sentiamus. Alii autem, quibus ego assentior, cum a philosophis compluribus permulta dicantur cur nec voluptas in bonis sit numeranda nec in malis dolor, non existimant oportere nimium nos causae confidere, sed et argumentandum et accurate disserendum et rationibus conquisitis de voluptate et dolore disputandum putant.

[32] Sed ut perspiciatis unde omnis iste natus error sit voluptatem accusantium doloremque laudantium, totam rem aperiam eaque ipsa quae ab illo inventore veritatis et quasi architecto beatae

fashion and say that it's not enough to claim that what is good and evil is determined by sense perception; our rational mind, too, can grasp that pleasure is to be sought for its own sake and pain to be avoided. So they maintain that our minds have a natural and inborn notion by which we know to seek out the one and reject the other. But others (and I'm in agreement with them) reckon that we shouldn't be too confident in our case, given that many philosophers have marshaled many arguments why pleasure shouldn't count as a good and pain as an evil. Therefore, they think that in discussing pleasure and pain, we need to offer proof, stringent arguments, and well-calibrated reasoning.

[32] But so that you can understand where people who accuse pleasure and praise pain get their wrong ideas, I'm going to be completely thorough and explain what has been said by

vitae dicta sunt explicabo. Nemo enim ipsam voluptatem quia voluptas sit aspernatur aut odit aut fugit, sed quia consequuntur magni dolores eos qui ratione voluptatem sequi nesciunt. Neque porro quisquam est qui dolorem ipsum, quia dolor sit, amet consectetur adipisci velit, sed quia non numquam eiusmodi tempora incidunt ut labore et dolore magnam aliquam quaerat voluptatem. Ut enim ad minima veniam, quis nostrum exercitationem ullam corporis suscipit laboriosam, nisi ut aliquid ex ea commodi consequatur? Quis autem vel eum iure reprehenderit qui in ea voluptate velit esse quam nihil molestiae consequatur, vel illum qui dolorem eum fugiat quo voluptas nulla pariatur?

[33] At vero eos et accusamus et iusto odio dignissimos ducimus qui blanditiis praesentium voluptatum deleniti atque corrupti quos dolores

Epicurus, that discoverer of truth and, so to speak, architect of the happy life. No one disdains, hates, or avoids pleasure simply because it is pleasure, but because those who don't know how to pursue pleasure in a rational way end up in a lot of pain. Likewise, no one loves, pursues, or seeks out pain simply because it is pain, but because not infrequently one finds oneself in circumstances where one pursues some great pleasure by means of toil and pain. To use a banal example, who of us would undertake any strenuous physical exercise except to get some benefit from it? But who can rightly blame someone who wants to experience the kind of pleasure that doesn't lead to any trouble, or otherwise someone who avoids the kind of pain that doesn't cause any pleasure?

[33] By contrast, we blame and rightly consider worthy of the greatest disapproval those who—pampered and corrupted by the seductions

et quas molestias excepturi sint obcaecati cupiditate non provident, similique sunt in culpa qui officia deserunt mollitia animi, id est laborum et dolorum fuga. Et harum quidem rerum facilis est et expedita distinctio. Nam libero tempore, cum soluta nobis est eligendi optio cumque nihil impedit quominus id quod maxime placeat facere possimus, omnis voluptas assumenda est, omnis dolor repellendus. Temporibus autem quibusdam et aut officiis debitis aut rerum necessitatibus saepe eveniet ut et voluptates repudiandae sint et molestiae non recusandae. itaque earum rerum hic tenetur a sapiente delectus, ut aut reiciendis voluptatibus maiores alias consequatur aut perferendis doloribus asperiores repellat.

(. . .)

of present pleasures—fail to anticipate what pains and annoyances they're creating for themselves, blinded as they are by their desires. Likewise, we fault those who abandon their duties out of a weakness of spirit—that is, in order to avoid toil and pain. And the difference between those two scenarios can be very easily explained. When we are at leisure and free to choose, and when there is nothing to prevent us from doing what we would most like to do, then every pleasure should be taken, every pain rejected. But in certain circumstances, when duty calls or some necessity arises, it will often happen that we have to reject pleasures and undergo trouble. And in this situation, wise people will have to make a choice, so that by rejecting some pleasures, they can achieve other and greater ones, or by going through some pains, they can avoid worse ones.

(. . .)

[37] Non enim hanc solam sequimur quae suavitate aliqua naturam ipsam movet et cum iucunditate quadam percipitur sensibus, sed maximam voluptatem illam habemus quae percipitur omni dolore detracto. Nam quoniam, cum privamur dolore, ipsa liberatione et vacuitate omnis molestiae gaudemus, omne autem id quo gaudemus voluptas est, ut omne quo offendimur dolor, doloris omnis privatio recte nominata est voluptas. Ut enim, cum cibo et potione fames sitisque depulsa est, ipsa detractio molestiae consecutionem affert voluptatis, sic in omni re doloris amotio successionem efficit voluptatis.

[38] Itaque non placuit Epicuro medium esse quiddam inter dolorem et voluptatem; illud enim ipsum quod quibusdam medium videretur, cum omni dolore careret, non modo voluptatem esse,

[37] And we don't just pursue the kind of pleasure that with a certain sweetness speaks directly to our nature and is perceived by the senses with delight. Instead, we consider the greatest pleasure the one we experience once all pain has been removed. For when we are freed from pain, we rejoice in this very liberation and the freedom from discomfort. But since everything in which we rejoice is pleasure (just as everything that hurts us is pain), the absence of all pain is rightly called pleasure. So, for example, when food and drink drive away hunger and thirst, the removal of discomfort itself leads to pleasure. Similarly, in every situation the departure of pain causes the arrival of pleasure.

[38] And this is why Epicurus doesn't think there is an intermediate state between pain and pleasure. For what some people believe is such an intermediate state—namely, the absence of

verum etiam summam voluptatem. Quisquis enim sentit quem ad modum sit affectus, eum necesse est aut in voluptate esse aut in dolore. Omnis autem privatione doloris putat Epicurus terminari summam voluptatem, ut postea variari voluptas distinguique possit, augeri amplificarique non possit.

[39] At etiam Athenis, ut e patre audiebam facete et urbane Stoicos irridente, statua est in Ceramico Chrysippi sedentis porrecta manu, quae manus significet illum in hac esse rogatiuncula delectatum:

Numquidnam manus tua sic affecta, quem ad
modum affecta nunc est, desiderat?
—Nihil sane.
At, si voluptas esset bonum, desideraret.

pain—that isn't just pleasure, but indeed the greatest pleasure. All people who are aware of their current experience must by necessity be either in pleasure or in pain. And Epicurus thinks that the greatest pleasure cannot be extended beyond the removal of all pain; afterward, you can come up with variations of pleasure, but you can't increase it any further.

[39] But my father—cleverly and wittily making fun of the Stoics—told me that in the Kerameikos in Athens, there is a statue of Chrysippus.[2] He is sitting there with his hand stretched out, a reference to the following little dialogue, in which he used to delight:

Your hand, in its present state, does it desire anything?

—Nothing at all.

But if pleasure were a good, it would desire pleasure.

—Ita credo.

Non est igitur voluptas bonum.

Hoc ne statuam quidem dicturam pater aiebat, si loqui posset. Conclusum est enim contra Cyrenaicos satis acute, nihil ad Epicurum. Nam si ea sola voluptas esset quae quasi titillaret sensus, ut ita dicam, et ad eos cum suavitate afflueret et illaberetur, nec manus esse contenta posset nec ulla pars vacuitate doloris sine iucundo motu voluptatis. Sin autem summa voluptas est, ut Epicuro placet, nihil dolere, primum tibi recte, Chrysippe, concessum est nihil desiderare manum, cum ita esset affecta, secundum non recte, si voluptas esset bonum, fuisse desideraturam. Idcirco enim non desideraret, quia quod dolore caret id in voluptate est.

—I think so.

Therefore, pleasure is not a good.

As my father said: not even a statue would talk like this if it could speak! It's a pretty good argument against the Cyrenaics, but it has no force against Epicurus.[3] Yes, if there existed only the kind of pleasure that tickles the senses, as it were, by flooding them with sweetness, then neither the hand nor any other body part would be satisfied by the absence of pain without the presence of the delightful stimulation of pleasure. But if, as Epicurus says, the greatest pleasure consists in experiencing no pain, then, Chrysippus, we'll concede your first point, that the hand in its present state doesn't desire anything. But you're wrong on the second point, that if pleasure were a good, the hand would desire pleasure. No: it would not desire anything,

[40] Extremum autem esse bonorum voluptatem ex hoc facillime perspici potest. Constituamus aliquem magnis multis perpetuis fruentem et animo et corpore voluptatibus nullo dolore nec impediente nec impendente: quem tandem hoc statu praestabiliorem aut magis expetendum possimus dicere? Inesse enim necesse est in eo qui ita sit affectus et firmitatem animi nec mortem nec dolorem timentis, quod mors sensu careat, dolor in longinquitate levis, in gravitate brevis soleat esse, ut eius magnitudinem celeritas, diuturnitatem allevatio consoletur. [41] Ad ea cum accedit ut neque divinum numen horreat nec praeteritas voluptates effluere patiatur earumque assidua recordatione laetetur, quid est quod huc possit, quo melius sit, accedere?

because whatever is free from pain is in fact in pleasure.

[40] And that pleasure is the greatest good can be easily understood from the following scenario. Let's picture someone who in mind and body is enjoying a great many uninterrupted pleasures without any pain either present or on the horizon. What state could we call preferable to this or more desirable? For by necessity a person in this condition is also firm of spirit and fears neither pain nor death: death, because it lacks sense perception; pain, because if it lasts for a long time, it is typically light, and if it is severe, it tends to be short (so short duration is the upside of severity, lightness the upside of long duration). [41] And if, in addition, the person neither shudders at the thought of the divine nor allows past pleasures to evaporate, but instead keeps rejoicing in their memory, what else

Statue contra aliquem confectum tantis animi corporisque doloribus quanti in hominem maximi cadere possunt, nulla spe proposita fore levius aliquando, nulla praeterea neque praesenti nec expectata voluptate: quid eo miserius dici aut fingi potest? Quodsi vita doloribus referta maxime fugienda est, summum profecto malum est vivere cum dolore; cui sententiae consentaneum est ultimum esse bonorum eum voluptate vivere. Nec enim habet nostra mens quicquam aliud ubi consistat tamquam in extremo, omnesque et metus et aegritudines ad dolorem referuntur, nec praeterea est res ulla, quae sua natura aut sollicitare possit aut angere.

[42] Praeterea et appetendi et refugiendi et omnino rerum gerendarum initia proficiscuntur aut a voluptate aut a dolore. Quod cum ita sit,

could be added to this to make their condition even better?

On the other side, let's posit someone consumed by the greatest mental and physical pains that can happen to a human being, without any hope that things could ever get better, and furthermore without any pleasure, either present or anticipated. What could we describe or imagine that would be more miserable than this? And if a life full of pain is thus to be avoided at all costs, then indeed living in pain is the greatest evil. From this it follows that the greatest good is living in pleasure. For our mind cannot imagine anything beyond this: all fears and anxieties have to do with pain, and other than that, there is nothing that can distress or upset us in its own right.

[42] In addition, our motivations for seeking or avoiding things, or for doing anything at all, arise from either pleasure or pain. And since this

perspicuum est omnis rectas res atque laudabilis eo referri ut cum voluptate vivatur. Quoniam autem id est vel summum bonorum vel ultimum vel extremum—quod Graeci τέλος nominant—, quod ipsum nullam ad aliam rem, ad id autem res referuntur omnes, fatendum est summum esse bonum iucunde vivere.

Id qui in una virtute ponunt et splendore nominis capti quid natura postulet non intellegunt, errore maximo, si Epicurum audire voluerint, liberabuntur. Istae enim vestrae eximiae pulchraeque virtutes nisi voluptatem efficerent, quis eas aut laudabilis aut expetendas arbitraretur? Ut enim medicorum scientiam non ipsius artis sed bonae valetudinis causa probamus, et gubernatoris ars, quia bene navigandi rationem habet, utilitate non arte laudatur, sic sapientia, quae ars vivendi putanda est, non expeteretur si nihil efficeret: nunc expetitur quod est tamquam artifex conquirendae

is so, it is obvious that all right and praiseworthy actions are directed at living in pleasure. And since the greatest, last, or final good (what the Greeks call the *telos*) is what is directed at nothing else, while all things are directed at it, therefore it must be admitted that the greatest good is to live pleasurably.

Those who think the greatest good consists in virtue as such and—deluded by such a splendid word—don't understand what nature demands would be freed from this huge error if only they would listen to Epicurus.[4] Those amazingly beautiful virtues of yours, who would consider them laudable or choice-worthy if they didn't bring about pleasure? We appreciate the knowledge of doctors not for the sake of science but for the sake of good health, and the skill of a helmsman who knows how to steer well is praised on account of its practical usefulness,

et comparandae voluptatis. [43] (Quam autem ego dicam voluptatem, iam videtis, ne invidia verbi labefactetur oratio mea.) Nam cum ignoratione rerum bonarum et malarum maxime hominum vita vexetur, ob eumque errorem et voluptatibus maximis saepe priventur et durissimis animi doloribus torqueantur, sapientia est adhibenda quae et terroribus cupiditatibusque detractis et omnium falsarum opinionum temeritate derepta certissimam se nobis ducem praebeat ad voluptatem.

Sapientia enim est una quae maestitiam pellat ex animis, quae nos exhorrescere metu non sinat. Qua praeceptrice in tranquillitate vivi potest

not its theoretical understanding. Similarly, people wouldn't strive for wisdom—which should be considered the art of life—if it had no effect; the reason they do try to attain it is because it is, so to speak, the craft of seeking and procuring pleasure. [43] (You know by now what kind of "pleasure" I mean—not to let people's prejudice against the term undermine my speech.) Human life suffers greatly from the fact that people don't know what is good or bad, and because of this ignorance they're often deprived of the greatest pleasures and vexed by the harshest mental pains. Therefore, we must employ wisdom, which removes fears and desires, tears away all our unexamined false opinions, and acts as our surest guide to pleasure.

Wisdom is the only thing that drives sadness from the mind, that prevents us from shuddering in fear. Following the precepts of wisdom, we can

omnium cupiditatum ardore restincto. Cupiditates enim sunt insatiabiles, quae non modo singulos homines, sed universas familias evertunt, totam etiam labefactant saepe rem publicam. [44] Ex cupiditatibus odia discidia discordiae seditiones bella nascuntur, nec eae se foris solum iactant nec tantum in alios caeco impetu incurrunt, sed intus etiam in animis inclusae inter se dissident atque discordant, ex quo vitam amarissimam necesse est effici, ut sapiens solum amputata circumcisaque inanitate omni et errore naturae finibus contentus sine aegritudine possit et sine metu vivere.

[45] Quae est enim aut utilior aut ad bene vivendum aptior partitio quam illa qua est usus Epicurus? Qui unum genus posuit earum cupiditatum quae essent et naturales et necessariae, alterum quae naturales essent nec tamen necessariae,

live in inner peace and extinguish all burning desires. For desires are insatiable and ruin not just individuals but entire families, and often even destabilize the commonwealth. [44] From desires arise hate, quarrels, discord, uprisings, and war. But desires don't just rage outside and attack others with blind aggression; hidden within the mind itself, they're at variance and fight against each other, with the necessary result that life turns into a nightmare. Therefore, only the wise person—the one who has completely cut away every empty opinion and every error, and who is content to remain within the boundaries of nature—is able to live without anxiety and fear.

[45] For what is more helpful or suited to the happy life than the division of desires proposed by Epicurus? He says that the first kind are those pleasures that are both natural and necessary; the second kind those that are natural but

tertium quae nec naturales nec necessariae. Quarum ea ratio est ut necessariae nec opera multa nec impensa expleantur; ne naturales quidem multa desiderant, propterea quod ipsa natura divitias quibus contenta sit et parabilis et terminatas habet; inanium autem cupiditatum nec modus ullus nec finis inveniri potest. [46] Quodsi vitam omnem perturbari videmus errore et inscientia, sapientiamque esse solam quae nos a libidinum impetu et a formidinum terrore vindicet et ipsius fortunae modice ferre doceat iniurias et omnis monstret vias quae ad quietem et ad tranquillitatem ferant, quid est cur dubitemus dicere et sapientiam propter voluptates expetendam et insipientiam propter molestias esse fugiendam?

[47] Eademque ratione ne temperantiam quidem propter se expetendam esse dicemus, sed

not necessary; and the third those that are neither natural nor necessary. The way this works is that the necessary desires can be fulfilled without much effort or cost; the natural ones don't ask for much either, because nature itself supplies the riches with which it is satisfied, and they're easy to procure and have their limits. The empty desires, by contrast, know no limit or end. [46] So we see that all life is disturbed by error and ignorance, and that wisdom alone frees us from the onslaught of desires and the terror of fears, teaches us to bear patiently the injuries of fortune, and shows us all the paths that lead to peace and tranquility. So why should we hesitate to assert that wisdom is to be sought on account of pleasure, and ignorance to be avoided on account of discomfort?

[47] In the same way, we'll say that not even moderation is to be sought for its own sake, but

quia pacem animis afferat et eos quasi concordia quadam placet ac leniat. Temperantia est enim quae in rebus aut expetendis aut fugiendis ut rationem sequamur monet. Nec enim satis est iudicare quid faciendum non faciendumve sit, sed stare etiam oportet in eo quod sit iudicatum. Plerique autem, quod tenere atque servare id quod ipsi statuerunt non possunt, victi et debilitati obiecta specie voluptatis tradunt se libidinibus constringendos nec quid eventurum sit provident, ob eamque causam propter voluptatem et parvam et non necessariam et quae vel aliter pararetur et qua etiam carere possent sine dolore tum in morbos gravis, tum in damna, tum in dedecora incurrunt, saepe etiam legum iudiciorumque poenis obligantur.

because it brings peace to the mind, and calms and soothes it with a certain harmony. For it is moderation that tells us to follow reason in everything we seek or avoid. It's not enough to reach a judgment about what one should or should not do, but one also needs to stick to the judgment one has made. But because many people are unable to adhere to their own decisions, they're weakened and defeated by any apparent pleasure that comes their way; thus, they surrender to licentiousness without any concern for the consequences. And therefore, all because of a small pleasure that isn't necessary, that they could procure another way or even painlessly do without, they end up sometimes with serious illness, sometimes with financial loss, and sometimes with a damaged reputation—and often they even incur the punishments of legal proceedings.

[48] Qui autem ita frui volunt voluptatibus ut nulli propter eas consequantur dolores, et qui suum iudicium retinent ne voluptate victi faciant id quod sentiant non esse faciendum, ii voluptatem maximam adipiscuntur praetermittenda voluptate. Idem etiam dolorem saepe perpetiuntur ne, si id non faciant, incidant in maiorem. Ex quo intellegitur nec intemperantiam propter se esse fugiendam temperantiamque expetendam non quia voluptates fugiat, sed quia maiores consequatur.

[49] Eadem fortitudinis ratio reperietur. Nam neque laborum perfunctio neque perpessio dolorum per se ipsa allicit, nec patientia nec assiduitas nec vigiliae nec ea ipsa quae laudatur industria, ne fortitudo quidem, sed ista sequimur ut sine cura metuque vivamus animumque et corpus, quantum efficere possimus, molestia liberemus. Ut enim

[48] But those who wish to enjoy pleasure without any subsequent pain, and who stick to their judgment and don't let themselves be overcome by pleasure to do what they know they shouldn't do, those people achieve the greatest pleasure—by forgoing pleasure. And they even often put up with pain, because if they didn't do so, they would meet with greater pain. And so we see that lack of moderation isn't to be shunned in and of itself, and that moderation is to be sought not because it avoids pleasures, but because it aims at greater ones.

[49] The same is true for courage. Undergoing toil and suffering pain aren't attractive as such, nor are endurance, perseverance, watchfulness, and energy, however much they get praised—and neither is courage itself. But we employ these things in order to live without worry and fear, and to free mind and body from discomfort

mortis metu omnis quietae vitae status perturbatur, et ut succumbere doloribus eosque humili animo inbecilloque ferre miserum est, ob eamque debilitatem animi multi parentes, multi amicos, nonnulli patriam, plerique autem se ipsos penitus perdiderunt, sic robustus animus et excelsus omni est liber cura et angore, cum et mortem contemnit, qua qui affecti sunt in eadem causa sunt qua ante quam nati, et ad dolores ita paratus est ut meminerit maximos morte finiri, parvos multa habere intervalla requietis, mediocrium nos esse dominos, ut si tolerabiles sint, feramus, si minus, animo aequo e vita, cum ea non placeat, tamquam e theatro exeamus. Quibus rebus intellegitur nec timiditatem ignaviamque vituperari nec fortitudinem patientiamque laudari suo nomine, sed illas reici quia dolorem pariant, has optari quia voluptatem.

to the extent that we can. For the fear of death perturbs any calm mode of life; surrendering to pain and reacting to it with a downcast and weak state of mind causes misery; and because of such feebleness of spirit many people ruin their parents or friends, some ruin their country, and quite a few utterly ruin themselves. By contrast, strong and lofty spirits are free from anxiety and disturbance. They despise death (our experience of which is just the same as our experience before birth[5]) and they're prepared for pains by remembering the following: strong pains end with death, weak pains have many interludes of respite, and those in the middle we can manage. If they're tolerable, we'll put up with them, but if they aren't, we'll leave life with a calm mind, just as we walk out of a play that we don't like. From all this, it is clear that we don't criticize timidity and cowardice, and praise courage and

[50] Iustitia restat, ut de omni virtute sit dictum; sed similia fere dici possunt. Ut enim sapientiam temperantiam fortitudinem copulatas esse docui cum voluptate, ut ab ea nullo modo nec divelli nec distrahi possint, sic de iustitia iudicandum est. Quae non modo numquam nocet cuiquam, sed contra semper affert aliquid cum vi sua atque natura quod tranquillat animos, tum spe nihil earum rerum defuturum quas natura non depravata desiderat. Et quem ad modum temeritas et libido et ignavia semper animum excruciant et semper sollicitant turbulentaeque sunt, sic improbitas si cuius in mente consedit, hoc ipso quod adest turbulenta est. Si vero molita quippiam est, quamvis occulte fecerit, numquam tamen id confidet fore semper occultum. Plerumque improborum

endurance, on their own account, but reject the former because they give rise to pain, and choose the latter because they provide pleasure.

[50] Justice is left, and then we'll have covered all the virtues. Here we can say similar things. I have demonstrated that wisdom, moderation, and courage are so closely linked to pleasure that they can't be severed or separated from it in any way, and we must conclude that the same is true for justice. Justice not only never harms anybody but also always brings benefits, both by its very own nature, which provides peace of mind, and by holding out the hope that there will be no lack of those things that nature (when it isn't corrupt) desires. And just as rashness, licentiousness, and cowardice continuously torture and disturb the mind and cause discomfort, thus wickedness disturbs people's mind through its very presence. And once it actually commits

facta primo suspicio insequitur, dein sermo atque fama, tum accusator, tum iudex; multi etiam, ut te consule, ipsi se indicaverunt.

[51] Quodsi qui satis sibi contra hominum conscientiam saepti esse et muniti videntur, deorum tamen horrent easque ipsas sollicitudines quibus eorum animi noctesque diesque exeduntur a diis immortalibus supplicii causa importari putant. Quae autem tanta ex improbis factis ad minuendas vitae molestias accessio potest fieri, quanta ad augendas, cum conscientia factorum, tum poena legum odioque civium? Et tamen in quibusdam neque pecuniae modus est neque honoris neque imperii nec libidinum nec epularum nec reliquarum cupiditatum, quas nulla praeda umquam

a crime, even if it does so in secret, it can never be confident that it will always remain hidden. The deeds of most criminals give rise first to suspicion, then to talk and gossip, then to prosecution, and finally to a trial. And many people even betray themselves, as happened in your consulship.[6]

[51] And those who think they have guarded and protected themselves well against being found out by human beings are still terrified of the gods and believe that the anxiety that eats at them day and night has been sent by the immortal gods as a punishment. What can anyone gain through wicked deeds that would diminish the discomforts of life rather than increase them, first through bad conscience and then through the punishment of the laws and the hatred of one's fellow citizens? But some people can never get enough of money, political office or power,

improbe parta minuit sed potius inflammat, ut coercendi magis quam dedocendi esse videantur.

[52] Invitat igitur vera ratio bene sanos ad iustitiam aequitatem fidem, neque homini infanti aut impotenti iniuste facta conducunt, qui nec facile efficere possit quod conetur nec optinere si effecerit, et opes vel fortunae vel ingenii liberalitati magis conveniunt, qua qui utuntur benevolentiam sibi conciliant et, quod aptissimum est ad quiete vivendum, caritatem, praesertim cum omnino nulla sit causa peccandi. [53] Quae enim cupiditates a natura proficiscuntur facile explentur sine ulla iniuria, quae autem inanes sunt, iis parendum non est. Nihil enim desiderabile concupiscunt, plusque in ipsa iniuria detrimenti est quam in iis rebus emolumenti quae pariuntur iniuria.

sex, parties, or any other desires—desires that are never diminished by ill-gotten gains but rather inflamed. Those people, it seems, must be constrained since they can't be untaught.

[52] Thus proper reasoning calls those who are truly sensible to justice, fairness, and good faith. Inarticulate and powerless people cannot profit from crime since they can't easily put their plans into action or carry them out successfully. Those who are blessed with resources and ingenuity will fare better by being generous; that way, they will make themselves liked and respected, which is most conducive to a quiet life—especially since there is absolutely no reason to do wrong. [53] For those desires that arise from nature are easily fulfilled without wrongdoing, while those that are empty shouldn't be heeded. They don't aim at anything desirable, and there is more disadvantage in wrongdoing

Itaque ne iustitiam quidem recte quis dixerit per se ipsam optabilem, sed quia iucunditatis vel plurimum afferat. Nam diligi et carum esse iucundum est propterea quia tutiorem vitam et voluptatum pleniorem efficit. Itaque non ob ea solum incommoda quae eveniunt inprobis fugiendam improbitatem putamus, sed multo etiam magis, quod, cuius in animo versatur, numquam sinit eum respirare, numquam adquiescere. [54] Quodsi ne ipsarum quidem virtutum laus, in qua maxime ceterorum philosophorum exultat oratio, reperire exitum potest nisi derigatur ad voluptatem, voluptas autem est sola quae nos vocet ad se et alliciat suapte natura, non potest esse dubium quin id sit summum atque extremum bonorum omnium, beateque vivere nihil aliud sit nisi cum voluptate vivere.

than advantage in those things one gains from wrongdoing.

Therefore not even justice can be said to be choice-worthy in its own right, but because it brings about many delightful things. Being loved and cherished is delightful because it makes life safer and fuller of pleasures. And thus we think that wickedness should be avoided not just because of the disadvantages that arise for the wicked, but even more so because wickedness never allows those whose minds it infests to draw a quiet breath. [54] So even that favorite topic of other philosophers, the exaltation of the virtues themselves, ultimately leads us to nothing else but to pleasure—while pleasure is the only thing that calls and draw us to itself by its very nature. And therefore there can be no doubt that this is the greatest and utmost of all goods, and that to live happily is nothing else but to live in pleasure.

[55] Huic certae stabilique sententiae quae sint coniuncta explicabo brevi. Nullus in ipsis error est finibus bonorum et malorum, id est in voluptate aut in dolore, sed in his rebus peccant cum e quibus haec efficiantur ignorant. Animi autem voluptates et dolores nasci fatemur e corporis voluptatibus et doloribus (itaque concedo quod modo dicebas, cadere causa si qui e nostris aliter existimant; quos quidem video esse multos sed imperitos); quamquam autem et laetitiam nobis voluptas animi et molestiam dolor afferat, eorum tamen utrumque et ortum esse e corpore et ad corpus referri, nec ob eam causam non multo maiores esse et voluptates et dolores animi quam corporis. Nam corpore nihil nisi praesens et quod adest sentire possumus, animo autem et praeterita et futura. Ut enim aeque doleamus cum corpore dolemus, fieri tamen permagna accessio potest si aliquod aeternum et infinitum impendere malum

[55] There is a corollary to this securely established axiom, which I will lay out briefly. There is no mistaking the greatest good and evil themselves—that is, pleasure and pain—but people make mistakes out of ignorance as to how these things come about. We maintain that the pleasures and pains of the mind arise from the pleasures and pains of the body (and I agree with what you said earlier, that if some Epicureans think otherwise, they can't make their case[7]; I see that there are many of those, but they're uninformed). Even though the pleasure of the mind brings us joy and the pain of the mind distress, both of them arise from the body and are concerned with the body. But this doesn't mean that the pleasures and pains of the mind aren't much greater than those of the body. With the body we can perceive only what is currently present, but with the mind also what is in the

nobis opinemur. Quod idem licet transferre in voluptatem, ut ea maior sit si nihil tale metuamus. [56] Iam illud quidem perspicuum est, maximam animi aut voluptatem aut molestiam plus aut ad beatam aut ad miseram vitam afferre momenti quam eorum utrumvis si aeque diu sit in corpore. Non placet autem detracta voluptate aegritudinem statim consequi, nisi in voluptatis locum dolor forte successerit, at contra gaudere nosmet omittendis doloribus, etiamsi voluptas ea quae sensum moveat nulla successerit, eoque intellegi potest quanta voluptas sit non dolere.

[57] Sed ut iis bonis erigimur quae expectamus, sic laetamur iis quae recordamur. Stulti autem malorum memoria torquentur, sapientes bona praeterita grata recordatione renovata delectant.

past and in the future. Of course, physical pain is properly pain, but it can be greatly increased if we think that some eternal and unending evil is threatening us. You can say the same about pleasure: it will be greater if we don't have any fear of this kind. [56] So it is quite clear that the greatest pleasure or discomfort of the mind contributes more to the happy or unhappy life, respectively, than the equivalent of each in the body, even if it is of equal duration. But we don't think that the removal of pleasure immediately leads to distress, unless pain has perchance taken its place; by contrast, we rejoice at the removal of pain, even if no physical pleasure has succeeded it. From this you can see how great a pleasure it is not to be in pain.

[57] And just as we are cheered up by expecting good things, so we take joy in those we remember. Fools agonize in the memory of bad things; wise people delight in past good things,

Est autem situm in nobis ut et adversa quasi perpetua oblivione obruamus et secunda iucunde ac suaviter meminerimus. Sed cum ea quae praeterierunt acri animo et attento intuemur, tum fit ut aegritudo sequatur si illa mala sint, laetitia si bona.

O praeclaram beate vivendi et apertam et simplicem et directam viam! Cum enim certe nihil homini possit melius esse quam vacare omni dolore et molestia perfruique maximis et animi et corporis voluptatibus, videtisne quam nihil praetermittatur quod vitam adiuvet, quo facilius id quod propositum est summum bonum consequamur? Clamat Epicurus, is quem vos nimis voluptatibus esse deditum dicitis, non posse iucunde vivi nisi sapienter honeste iusteque vivatur, nec sapienter honeste iuste, nisi iucunde.
(. . .)

brought back to life in grateful recollection. For we have the power to bury bad fortune in perpetual oblivion but remember good fortune with sweet delight. If we concentrate hard on what happened in the past, distress follows if it was bad, but joy if it was good.

What an excellent, obvious, easy, and direct way to happiness! It is clearly the case that nothing better can happen to a person than to be free from all pain and discomfort and to enjoy the greatest pleasures of mind and body—and you see how we have left off nothing that might help us in life to achieve the greatest good that we have posited? Epicurus, the man who you say is too much given to pleasures, declares loud and clear that one cannot live pleasantly without living wisely, morally, and justly, nor can one live wisely, morally, and justly without living pleasantly.

(. . .)

[65] Restat locus huic disputationi vel maxime necessarius de amicitia, quam, si voluptas summum sit bonum, affirmatis nullam omnino fore. De qua Epicurus quidem ita dicit, omnium rerum quas ad beate vivendum sapientia comparaverit nihil esse maius amicitia, nihil uberius, nihil iucundius. Nec vero hoc oratione solum, sed multo magis vita et factis et moribus comprobavit.

Quod quam magnum sit fictae veterum fabulae declarant, in quibus tam multis tamque variis ab ultima antiquitate repetitis tria vix amicorum paria reperiuntur, ut ad Orestem pervenias profectus a Theseo. At vero Epicurus una in domo, et ea quidem angusta, quam magnos quantaque amoris conspiratione consentientis tenuit amicorum greges! Quod fit etiam nunc ab Epicureis. Sed ad rem redeamus; de hominibus dici non necesse est.

[65] I still need to discuss another topic, and a very important one too: friendship. You claim that there will be no such thing as friendship if pleasure is the greatest good. Epicurus, by contrast, states that of all the things that wisdom has provided for happiness, nothing is greater, more productive, and more delightful than friendship. And he has given us proof of this not only in his words, but also and much more so in his life, actions, and character.

What a great thing friendship is is apparent from the myths of old. In all those many different stories going back to the deepest past, we can barely find three pairs of friends: there is no one between Theseus and Orestes.[8] But Epicurus in his own fairly small house had a great multitude of friends connected by an amazing bond of affection. The same is true of Epicureans still today. But let's return to the topic; there is no need to talk about individuals.

[66] Tribus igitur modis video esse a nostris de amicitia disputatum. Alii cum eas voluptates quae ad amicos pertinerent negarent esse per se ipsas tam expetendas quam nostras expeteremus (quo loco videtur quibusdam stabilitas amicitiae vacillare), tuentur tamen eum locum seque facile, ut mihi videtur, expediunt. Ut enim virtutes, de quibus ante dictum est, sic amicitiam negant posse a voluptate discedere. Nam cum solitudo et vita sine amicis insidiarum et metus plena sit, ratio ipsa monet amicitias comparare, quibus partis confirmatur animus et a spe pariendarum voluptatum seiungi non potest.

[67] Atque ut odia invidiae despicationes adversantur voluptatibus, sic amicitiae non modo fautrices fidelissimae sed etiam effectrices sunt voluptatum tam amicis quam sibi, quibus non

[66] As far as I can tell, Epicureans have put forth three theories concerning friendship.[9] The first group states that our friends' pleasures are not worthy of pursuit on their own account the way our own pleasures are—and that's where some people think that friendship will founder. But those Epicureans stick to their guns and, in my opinion, extricate themselves easily. For just as is true of the virtues, which I discussed earlier,[10] so friendship (they say) cannot be divorced from pleasure. Since a solitary life without friends is full of pitfalls and fears, reason itself impels us to seek friendships. Once we have those, our mind gains confidence and the lasting hope of securing pleasures.

[67] And just as hatred, envy, and contempt stand in the way of pleasures, so too friendship not only favors pleasures but also brings them about, both for our friends and for ourselves.

solum praesentibus fruuntur, sed etiam spe eriguntur consequentis ac posteri temporis. Quod quia nullo modo sine amicitia firmam et perpetuam iucunditatem vitae tenere possumus neque vero ipsam amicitiam tueri nisi aeque amicos et nosmet ipsos diligamus, idcirco et hoc ipsum efficitur in amicitia, et amicitia cum voluptate conectitur. Nam et laetamur amicorum laetitia aeque atque nostra et pariter dolemus angoribus.

[68] Quocirca eodem modo sapiens erit affectus erga amicum quo in se ipsum, quosque labores propter suam voluptatem susciperet, eosdem suscipiet propter amici voluptatem. Quaeque de virtutibus dicta sunt, quem ad modum eae semper voluptatibus inhaererent, eadem de amicitia dicenda sunt. Praeclare enim Epicurus his paene verbis: "Eadem," inquit, "sapientia confirmavit animum ne quod aut sempiternum aut diuturnum

And we don't just enjoy those in the present, but are also heartened by our hopes for the times to come. Without friendship, we cannot possibly maintain a stable and lasting delight in life, and we cannot keep friendship itself alive if we do not love our friends as much as we love ourselves. That is what happens in friendship, and friendship is bound up with pleasure. For we rejoice in the joy of our friends as in our own, and likewise suffer at their distress.

[68] Therefore the wise will have the same disposition toward their friends as toward themselves, and they will make the same efforts for the pleasure of their friends that they make for their own pleasure. And what I have said about the virtues, how they are always linked to pleasures, the same can be said about friendship as well. Epicurus put it very well, more or less in these words: "The realization that in this

timeret malum quae perspexit in hoc ipso vitae spatio amicitiae praesidium esse firmissimum."

[69] Sunt autem quidam Epicurei timidiores paulo contra vestra convicia, sed tamen satis acuti, qui verentur ne, si amicitiam propter nostram voluptatem expetendam putemus, tota amicitia quasi claudicare videatur. Itaque primos congressus copulationesque et consuetudinum instituendarum voluntates fieri propter voluptatem; cum autem usus progrediens familiaritatem effecerit, tum amorem efflorescere tantum ut, etiamsi nulla sit utilitas ex amicitia, tamen ipsi amici propter se ipsos amentur. Etenim si loca, si fana, si urbes, si gymnasia, si campum, si canes, si equos, si ludicra exercendi aut venandi consuetudine adamare solemus, quanto id in hominum consuetudine facilius fieri poterit et iustius?

lifetime friendship affords the strongest protection is what allows wisdom to give our minds the strength not to fear any everlasting evil."

[69] There are, however, certain Epicureans who are mildly intimidated by your attacks, though still sharp enough. They fear that, if we think that friendship is to be sought for the sake of pleasure, then friendship seems, as it were, completely lame. They therefore posit that we first approach, get together, and want to spend time with our friends for the sake of pleasure. Once we have grown close to them over time, however, then an affection arises that is so great that, even if the friendship is not at all useful to us, we nevertheless love our friends for themselves. Since habit makes us develops affection for places, temples, cities, gyms, exercise grounds, dogs, horses, gladiatorial shows, and wild beast

[70] Sunt autem qui dicant foedus esse quoddam sapientium, ut ne minus amicos quam se ipsos diligant. Quod et posse fieri intellegimus et saepe etiam videmus, et perspicuum est nihil ad iucunde vivendum reperiri posse quod coniunctione tali sit aptius. Quibus ex omnibus iudicari potest non modo non impediri rationem amicitiae si summum bonum in voluptate ponatur, sed sine hoc institutionem omnino amicitiae non posse reperiri.

hunts, why shouldn't the same happen—and more easily and with greater justification—when we grow used to a person?

[70] There are also those who say that the wise make a sort of pact not to love their friends less than themselves. We recognize that this is possible and even often see it happen; it is clear that there is nothing more conducive to happiness than this kind of bond. From all this, we can conclude not only that by placing the greatest good in pleasure, we do not imperil the concept of friendship, but also that without doing so, we cannot find any basis for friendship at all.

[3] Omnis autem in quaerendo quae via quadam et ratione habetur oratio praescribere primum debet, ut quibusdam in formulis EA RES AGETUR, ut inter quos disseritur conveniat quid sit id de quo disseratur. [4] Hoc positum in Phaedro a Platone probavit Epicurus sensitque in omni disputatione id fieri oportere. Sed quod proximum fuit non vidit. Negat enim definiri rem placere, sine quo fieri interdum non potest ut inter eos qui ambigunt conveniat quid sit id de quo agatur, velut in hoc ipso de quo nunc disputamus. Quaerimus enim

BOOK 2
The Problems with Pleasure

Responding to Torquatus, Cicero provides a critique of Epicureanism.

[3] Any investigation that proceeds in a methodical and rational manner must first define its topic—as we indicate with a phrase like *in re*[1]—so that the discussants can agree on what it is they're debating. [4] That's what Plato said in the *Phaedrus*,[2] and Epicurus approved and thought this should be done in any discussion. But he didn't see the next step. He claims that he doesn't like to define things, but if you don't do that, then sometimes people who have an argument cannot agree on what it is they're arguing about.

finem bonorum. Possumusne hic scire qualis sit nisi contulerimus inter nos, cum finem bonorum dixerimus, quid finis, quid etiam sit ipsum bonum? [5] atqui haec patefactio quasi rerum opertarum, cum quid quidque sit aperitur, definitio est.

qua tu etiam imprudens utebare non numquam. Nam hunc ipsum sive finem sive extremum sive ultimum definiebas id esse quo omnia, quae recte fierent, referrentur neque id ipsum usquam referretur. Praeclare hoc quidem. Bonum ipsum etiam quid esset fortasse, si opus fuisset, definisses aut quod esset natura appetendum aut quod prodesset aut quod iuvaret aut quod liberet modo. Nunc idem, nisi molestum est, quoniam tibi non omnino displicet definire et id facis cum vis, velim definias quid sit voluptas, de quo omnis haec quaestio est.

And that's true for our discussion here. We are looking for the greatest good. How can we know what it is if we haven't first determined the following among ourselves: when we speak of the "greatest good," what do we mean by "greatest" and what do we mean by "good" itself? [5] To bring into the open, if you will, things that have been hidden and to show their nature, that's definition.

But you weren't careful and sometimes even used a definition yourself. You defined the "greatest" or "final" or "ultimate" as that to which all correct actions are directed but that itself isn't directed anywhere else. That's very good. And in a pinch, you could perhaps also have defined the "good" as that which is by nature choice-worthy, or that which is useful, or that which is pleasant, or simply that which is appealing. Now if you don't mind, since you aren't entirely opposed to defining things and

[6] Quis, quaeso, inquit, est qui quid sit voluptas nesciat, aut qui quo magis id intellegat, definitionem aliquam desideret?

Me ipsum esse dicerem, inquam, nisi mihi viderer habere bene cognitam voluptatem et satis firme conceptam animo atque comprehensam. Nunc autem dico ipsum Epicurum nescire et in eo nutare, eumque qui crebro dicat diligenter oportere exprimi quae vis subiecta sit vocibus non intellegere interdum quid sonet haec vox voluptatis, id est quae res huic voci subiciatur.

Tum ille ridens: Hoc vero, inquit, optimum, ut is qui finem rerum expetendarum voluptatem esse dicat, id extremum, id ultimum bonorum, id ipsum quid et quale sit, nesciat! Atqui, inquam,

do it when you feel like it, please define what "pleasure" is, since that's what this whole discussion is about.

[6] Come on, he said, who is there who doesn't know what pleasure is, or who needs some definition to understand it better?

I would say "I myself," I said, if I didn't think I already had an understanding of pleasure, and a very clear conception of it in my mind. But I maintain that Epicurus doesn't know it and keeps drifting off on this point. Though he often says that one needs to express with precision the reality that lies behind words, he himself sometimes doesn't understand what the word "pleasure" means, that is, what reality lies behind the word.

He laughed and said, that's really a great joke, that the man who says that pleasure is the goal of all our choices shouldn't know what this last and final good itself is like!

aut Epicurus quid sit voluptas aut omnes mortales, qui ubique sunt, nesciunt.

Quonam, inquit, modo?

Quia voluptatem hanc esse sentiunt omnes quam sensus accipiens movetur et iucunditate quadam perfunditur.

[7] Quid ergo? Istam voluptatem, inquit, Epicurus ignorat?

Non semper, inquam; nam interdum nimis etiam novit, quippe qui testificetur ne intellegere quidem se posse ubi sit aut quod sit ullum bonum praeter illud quod cibo et potione et aurium delectatione et obscena voluptate capiatur. An haec ab eo non dicuntur?

Quasi vero me pudeat, inquit, istorum, aut non possim quem ad modum ea dicantur ostendere!

Ego vero non dubito, inquam, quin facile possis, nec est quod te pudeat sapienti adsentiri qui

Well, I said, either Epicurus doesn't know what pleasure is, or all mortals everywhere don't know it.

How so?

Because all people think that pleasure is a sensation that impacts our perception and pervades it with a certain delight.

[7] So what? Is Epicurus ignorant of this kind of pleasure?

Not always, I said. Sometimes he even knows it all too well, as when he declares that he can't even understand what good there can be anywhere except the one experienced through food and drink and delightful sounds and sex. Or aren't these his words?

As if I were ashamed of these words, he said, or couldn't explain their meaning!

I have no doubt, I said, that you could easily do so, and there is no reason to be ashamed for

se unus, quod sciam, sapientem profiteri sit ausus. Nam Metrodorum non puto ipsum professum sed, cum appellaretur ab Epicuro, repudiare tantum beneficium noluisse; septem autem illi non suo sed populorum suffragio omnium nominati sunt. [8] Verum hoc loco sumo verbis his eandem certe vim voluptatis Epicurum nosse quam ceteros. omnes enim iucundum motum quo sensus hilaretur Graece ἡδονήν, Latine voluptatem vocant.

Quid est igitur, inquit, quod requiras?

Dicam, inquam, et quidem discendi causa magis quam quo te aut Epicurum reprehensum velim.

Ego quoque, inquit, didicerim libentius, si quid attuleris, quam te reprehenderim.

agreeing with a wise man—the only one, as far as I know, who dared to declare himself wise. For I think Metrodorus didn't make this claim for himself; however, when Epicurus called him wise, he didn't want to reject such a great compliment.[3] As for the Seven Sages, they got their nickname not by their own judgment but by that of the people.[4] [8] Anyway, I assume from this quotation that there Epicurus understands pleasure the same way as everyone else. For everyone calls that delightful stimulation that cheers the senses *hēdonē* in Greek and pleasure (*voluptas*) in Latin.

So what else do you want, he said?

I'll tell you, I said, and I'll do so because I want to learn, not because I want to criticize you or Epicurus.

I too, he said, would rather learn something, if you have something to offer, than criticize you.

Tenesne igitur, inquam, Hieronymus Rhodius quid dicat esse summum bonum, quo putet omnia referri oportere?

Teneo, inquit, finem illi videri nihil dolere.

Quid? Idem iste, inquam, de voluptate quid sentit?

[9] Negat esse eam, inquit, propter se expetendam.

Aliud igitur esse censet gaudere, aliud non dolere.

Et quidem, inquit, vehementer errat; nam, ut paulo ante docui, augendae voluptatis finis est doloris omnis amotio.

Non dolere, inquam, istud quam vim habeat postea videro; aliam vero vim voluptatis esse,

Are you aware, I asked, what Hieronymus of Rhodes thinks the greatest good is, the one to which he thinks everything else should be directed[5]?

Sure, he said, he thinks the greatest good is being free from pain.

All right. And what does he think about pleasure?

[9] He says that it isn't worthy of being sought for itself.

So he thinks pleasure is one thing and freedom from pain another.

And indeed, Torquatus said, that's where he's sorely mistaken. For as I explained a little while ago, the end point of the increase of pleasure is the removal of all pain.

I'll leave the question of what freedom from pain means until later, I said. But unless you're

aliam nihil dolendi, nisi valde pertinax fueris, concedas necesse est.

Atqui reperies, inquit, in hoc quidem pertinacem; dici enim nihil potest verius.

Estne, quaeso, inquam, sitienti in bibendo voluptas?

Quis istud possit, inquit, negare?

Eademne, quae restincta siti?

Immo alio genere; restincta enim sitis stabilitatem voluptatis habet, inquit, illa autem voluptas ipsius restinctionis in motu est.

Cur igitur, inquam, res tam dissimiles eodem nomine appellas?

[10] Quid paulo ante, inquit, dixerim nonne meministi, cum omnis dolor detractus esset, variari, non augeri voluptatem?

really stubborn, you'll have to admit that in essence pleasure is one thing and freedom from pain another.

Well, that's where you will find me very stubborn then, he said. There is nothing more correct than our view of the matter.

Please, I said, does a thirsty person take pleasure in drinking?

Who can deny it?

And is it the same pleasure when the thirst has been quenched?

It's pleasure of a different kind: quenched thirst is a static pleasure, while the quenching is a pleasure in motion.

So why, I said, are you using the same word for two things that are so different?

[10] Don't you remember what I said a little while ago, that when all pain has been removed, pleasure can be varied but not increased?

Memini vero, inquam; sed tu istuc dixti bene Latine, parum plane. Varietas enim Latinum verbum est, idque proprie quidem in disparibus coloribus dicitur, sed transfertur in multa disparia: varium poema, varia oratio, varii mores, varia fortuna, voluptas etiam varia dici solet cum percipitur e multis dissimilibus rebus dissimilis efficientibus voluptates. Eam si varietatem diceres, intellegerem, ut etiam non dicente te intellego: ista varietas quae sit non satis perspicio, quod ais cum dolore careamus, tum in summa voluptate nos esse, cum autem vescamur iis rebus quae dulcem motum afferant sensibus, tum esse in motu voluptatem, qui faciat varietatem voluptatum, sed non augeri illam non dolendi voluptatem, quam cur voluptatem appelles nescio.

I remember it well. The language of your words was clear, the meaning less so. "Variety" (*varietas*) is a Latin word that originally refers to different colors but can be transferred to many things of a heterogeneous character: a poem or a speech with variations, or a varied character or varied fortune. Pleasure, too, can be said to be varied if the experience of it arises from many different things that bring about different pleasures. If you were talking about this kind of variety, I would understand you (and that's what I take you to mean even though you aren't actually saying it), but I don't understand that other kind of variety. You say that when we are free from pain, we experience the greatest pleasure, but when we enjoy the kinds of things that cause sweet stimulation to the senses, that's pleasure in motion, which brings about a variety of pleasures. And the pleasure that consists in

[11] An potest, inquit, quicquam esse suavius quam nihil dolere?

Immo sit sane nihil melius, inquam, nondum enim id quaero; num propterea idem voluptas est, quod, ut ita dicam, indolentia?

Plane idem, inquit, et maxima quidem, qua fieri nulla maior potest.

Quid dubitas igitur, inquam, summo bono a te ita constituto ut id totum in non dolendo sit, id tenere unum, id tueri, id defendere? [12] Quid enim necesse est, tamquam meretricem in matronarum coetum, sic voluptatem in virtutum concilium adducere? Invidiosum nomen est, infame, suspectum. Itaque hoc frequenter dici solet a vobis, non intellegere nos quam dicat Epicurus voluptatem. Quod quidem mihi si quando dictum

the freedom from pain cannot be increased—but I don't understand why you are calling it a pleasure in the first place.

[11] Can anything, he said, be more pleasant than not to feel pain?

Let's even say there can be nothing better, I said, that's not yet the issue. But is pleasure therefore the same as painlessness?

Absolutely, he said, and that's in fact the greatest pleasure, the one that cannot be exceeded.

So if you have defined your greatest good in this way, that it consists entirely in not feeling pain, why don't you keep to it, stick to it, and defend it? [12] What need is there to bring "pleasure" into the set of virtues, like a prostitute into a gathering of married ladies? It's a disreputable word, a notorious and suspect one. And then you people like to claim over and over that we don't understand what Epicurus means

est (est autem dictum non parum saepe), etsi satis clemens sum in disputando, tamen interdum soleo subirasci. egone non intellego quid sit ἡδονή Graece, Latine voluptas? Utram tandem linguam nescio?

Deinde qui fit ut ego nesciam, sciant omnes quicumque Epicurei esse voluerunt? Quod vestri quidem vel optime disputant, nihil opus esse eum qui philosophus futurus sit scire litteras. Itaque ut maiores nostri ab aratro adduxerunt Cincinnatum illum ut dictator esset, sic vos de pagis omnibus colligitis bonos illos quidem viros sed certe non pereruditos. [13] Ergo illi intellegunt quid Epicurus dicat, ego non intellego?

Ut scias me intellegere, primum idem esse dico voluptatem, quod ille ἡδονήν. Et quidem saepe quaerimus verbum Latinum par Graeco et quod

by pleasure. When I'm told this (and I'm told this fairly frequently), I sometimes get a little bit annoyed, though I'm usually fairly mild-mannered in philosophical discussions. So I don't understand what *hēdonē* means in Greek and "pleasure" in Latin? Just which language is it I don't know?

And how come I don't know it, but all would-be Epicureans do? Of course, you people make that wonderful argument that in order to be a philosopher, you don't need any education. And just as our ancestors took Cincinnatus away from his plow to make him dictator,[6] so you collect from all over the countryside good folks who aren't exactly overeducated. [13] So they understand what Epicurus is saying, and I don't?

And to prove that I do understand, let me first point out that our "pleasure" means the same as Epicurus's *hēdonē*. We often search for a Latin

idem valeat: hic nihil fuit quod quaereremus. Nullum inveniri verbum potest quod magis idem declaret Latine quod Graece, quam declarat voluptas. Huic verbo omnes qui ubique sunt qui Latine sciunt duas res subiciunt, laetitiam in animo, commotionem suavem iucunditatis in corpore. Nam et ille apud Trabeam "voluptatem animi nimiam" laetitiam dicit eandem quam ille Caecilianus qui "omnibus laetitiis laetum" esse se narrat. Sed hoc interest quod voluptas dicitur etiam in animo (vitiosa res, ut Stoici putant, qui eam sic definiunt: sublationem animi sine ratione opinantis se magno bono frui), non dicitur laetitia nec gaudium in corpore.

[14] In eo autem voluptas omnium Latine loquentium more ponitur, cum percipitur ea quae

word equivalent to a Greek one, one that means the same thing. In this case, there was no need to search: no word can be found that more exactly signifies in Latin the same thing as in Greek than "pleasure." And by this word, anybody anywhere who knows Latin understands two things: joy in the mind and a sweet stimulation of delight in the body. For when that character of Trabea's talks about "excessive pleasure in the mind," he means the same kind of joy as the man in the play by Caecilius who says that he's "overjoyed by joys."[7] The difference is that we can talk about pleasure in the mind (something the Stoics think is a vice, defining it as "the elation of the mind when people think without cause that they're enjoying a great good"[8]), but not about joy or cheer in the body.

[14] And in the usage of all Latin-speakers, "pleasure" is used when one feels the delight that

sensum aliquem moveat iucunditas. Hanc quoque iucunditatem, si vis, transfer in animum (iuvare enim in utroque dicitur, ex eoque iucundum), modo intellegas inter illum qui dicat

> Tanta laetitia auctus sum ut nihil constet

et eum qui

> Nunc demum mihi animus ardet,

quorum alter laetitia gestiat, alter dolore crucietur, esse illum medium qui nec laetetur nec angatur, itemque inter eum qui potiatur corporis expetitis voluptatibus et eum qui crucietur summis doloribus esse eum qui utroque careat.

stimulates one of the senses. And if you wish, we can transfer this delight to the mind, for we can use "feel delight" of both body and mind, and speak of what's "delightful." However, you must understand that if one person says,

> I'm so full of joy, I'm all agog,

and another,

> Now my mind is burning,[9]

in other words, if one is reveling in joy and the other is tortured by pain, that there also exists an intermediate state where one neither rejoices nor feels anguish. Likewise, in between the person who enjoys all desired physical pleasures and the one who is racked by the greatest pain, there is the one who is free of both.

[15] Satisne igitur videor vim verborum tenere, an sum etiam nunc vel Graece loqui vel Latine docendus? Et tamen vide ne, si ego non intellegam quid Epicurus loquatur, cum Graece, ut videor, luculenter sciam, sit aliqua culpa eius qui ita loquatur ut non intellegatur. Quod duobus modis sine reprehensione fit, si aut de industria facias, ut Heraclitus, cognomento qui σκοτεινός perhibetur, quia de natura nimis obscure memoravit, aut cum rerum obscuritas, non verborum, facit ut non intellegatur oratio, qualis est in Timaeo Platonis. Epicurus autem, ut opinor, nec non vult, si possit, plane et aperte loqui, nec de re obscura, ut physici, aut artificiosa, ut mathematici, sed de illustri et facili et iam in vulgus pervagata loquitur.

[15] So do I appear to know the meaning of words, or do I still need to learn either Greek or Latin? You better be careful: if I don't understand what Epicurus is saying, even though I clearly know Greek perfectly well, perhaps it is somehow his fault if he speaks in a way that is hard to understand. There are two contexts in which it is acceptable to do so. Either someone does it on purpose, like Heraclitus, who was called "the dark" because he spoke about nature in a very obscure fashion, or the obscurity of the subject matter, not of the words, renders the exposition hard to understand, as in Plato's *Timaeus*.[10] But Epicurus in my opinion aims at speaking plainly and clearly, and he isn't talking about an obscure subject matter (like natural philosophy) or a technical one (like mathematics), but about one that is well-known and easy and part of popular culture.

Quamquam non negatis nos intellegere quid sit voluptas, sed quid ille dicat. E quo efficitur, non ut nos non intellegamus quae vis sit istius verbi, sed ut ille suo more loquatur, nostrum neglegat. [16] Si enim idem dicit quod Hieronymus, qui censet summum bonum esse sine ulla molestia vivere, cur mavult dicere voluptatem quam vacuitatem doloris, ut ille facit, qui quid dicat intellegit? Sin autem voluptatem putat adiungendam eam quae sit in motu (sic enim appellat hanc dulcem, in motu, illam nihil dolentis, in stabilitate), quid tendit? Cum efficere non possit ut cuiquam qui ipse sibi notus sit, hoc est qui suam naturam sensumque perspexerit, vacuitas doloris et voluptas idem esse videatur. Hoc est vim afferre, Torquate, sensibus, extorquere ex animis cognitiones verborum, quibus inbuti sumus. Quis enim est qui non videat haec esse in natura rerum tria? unum, cum in voluptate sumus, alterum cum in dolore,

Still, your claim is not that we don't understand what pleasure is, but that we don't understand what Epicurus is saying. What follows from this is not that we don't know what that word means, but that Epicurus has his own way of talking that deviates from ours. [16] For if he means the same thing as Hieronymus, who thinks it's the greatest good to live without any distress, then why does he insist on calling this "pleasure" rather than "freedom from pain," as Hieronymus does, who understands his own words? But if he wants to add the kind of pleasure in motion (that's what he calls that sweet pleasure, "in motion," while the pleasure of not feeling pain is "at rest"), where is he going with that? He isn't going to get any folks who know themselves, that is, who understand their own nature and experience, to agree that freedom from pain and pleasure are the same thing. That

tertium hoc in quo nunc equidem sum, credo item vos, nec in dolore nec in voluptate; ut in voluptate sit qui epuletur, in dolore qui torqueatur. Tu autem inter haec tantam multitudinem hominum interiectam non vides nec laetantium nec dolentium?

[17] Non prorsus, inquit, omnisque qui sine dolore sint in voluptate, et ea quidem summa, esse dico.

Ergo in eadem voluptate eum qui alteri misceat mulsum ipse non sitiens, et eum qui illud sitiens bibat?

means doing violence to sense perception, Torquatus, and twisting from our minds the meanings of words, which are deeply ingrained. For who doesn't see that there are three natural states? The first, when we are in pleasure; the second, when we are in pain; and the third, the one in which I am right now, and I think you two as well, that is, neither in pain nor in pleasure. So the person who is at the dinner table is in pleasure; the one who is being tortured is in pain. But don't you see that between these extremes there exist an enormous number of people who are feeling neither pleasure nor pain?

[17] Not at all, he said. I maintain that all those who aren't in pain are in pleasure, and in the greatest one, too.

So the person who isn't thirsty and mixes a drink for someone else has the same pleasure as the one who is thirsty and drinks it?

Tum ille: Finem, inquit, interrogandi, si videtur.

(. . .)

[31] A primo, ut opinor, animantium ortu petitur origo summi boni. Simul atque natum animal est, gaudet voluptate et eam appetit ut bonum, aspernatur dolorem ut malum. De malis autem et bonis ab iis animalibus quae nondum depravata sint ait optime iudicari. Haec et tu ita posuisti, et verba vestra sunt. Quam multa vitiosa! Summum enim bonum et malum vagiens puer utra voluptate diiudicabit, stante an movente? Quoniam, si dis placet, ab Epicuro loqui discimus. Si stante, hoc natura videlicet vult, salvam esse se, quod concedimus; si movente, quod tamen dicitis, nulla turpis voluptas erit quae praetermittenda sit, et

At that point he said: Please, stop interrogating me!
(. . .)

Cicero stops questioning Torquatus and continues his critique.

[31] First of all, as far as I can tell, Epicurus seeks the origin of the greatest good in the birth of living beings. As soon as a creature is born, it rejoices in pleasure and pursues it as a good, and rejects pain as an evil. And he says that one can get the best idea about good and evil from creatures that have not yet been corrupted. That's how you put it, and in those very words. What an unsound argument! Judging by which kind of pleasure will a wailing infant decide on the greatest good and evil, the one "at rest" or the one "in motion" (since, god help us, we are now picking up Epicurean terminology)? If it's the

simul non proficiscitur animal illud modo natum a summa voluptate, quae est a te posita in non dolendo.

[32] Nec tamen argumentum hoc Epicurus a parvis petivit aut etiam a bestiis, quae putat esse specula naturae, ut diceret ab iis duce natura hanc voluptatem expeti nihil dolendi. Nec enim haec movere potest appetitum animi, nec ullum habet ictum quo pellat animum status hic non dolendi (itaque in hoc eodem peccat Hieronymus). At ille pellit qui permulcet sensum voluptate. Itaque Epicurus semper hoc utitur ut probet voluptatem natura expeti, quod ea voluptas quae in motu sit et parvos ad se alliciat et bestias, non illa stabilis, in qua tantum inest nihil dolere. Qui igitur

static pleasure, then that's indeed what nature wants—namely, to be safe—and I admit that. But if it's the moving kind, which is what you mean, then this is going to include every shameful pleasure—and in addition, that creature, just born, doesn't start from the greatest pleasure, which you claim consists in not feeling pain.

[32] But Epicurus didn't base his proof on beasts and babies (who he thinks are mirrors of nature) in order to show that, guided by nature, they pursue the pleasure of painlessness. For the mind can't be stimulated into craving the state of not feeling pain (that's a problem for Hieronymus, too)—only into craving the state that floods the senses with pleasure. And that's the one Epicurus is always referring to in order to prove that pleasure is sought by nature, because it's the pleasure in motion that lures beasts and babies, not the one at rest, which is simply the

convenit ab alia voluptate dicere naturam proficisci, in alia summum bonum ponere?

[33] Bestiarum vero nullum iudicium puto. Quamvis enim depravatae non sint, pravae tamen esse possunt. Ut bacillum aliud est inflexum et incurvatum de industria, aliud ita natum, sic ferarum natura non est illa quidem depravata mala disciplina, sed natura sua. Nec vero ut voluptatem expetat natura movet infantem, sed tantum ut se ipse diligat, ut integrum se salvumque velit. Omne enim animal, simul et ortum est, se ipsum et omnes partes suas diligit duasque quae maximae sunt in primis amplectitur, animum et corpus, deinde utriusque partes. Nam sunt et in animo praecipua quaedam et in corpore, quae cum leviter agnovit, tum discernere incipit, ut ea, quae prima data sunt natura appetat asperneturque contraria.

absence of pain. So how can you at the same time claim that nature starts from one kind of pleasure and maintain that the greatest good consists in another kind?

[33] Frankly, I don't think the judgment of beasts is worth anything. They may not be corrupted, but they can be corrupt. Just as one piece of wood has been bent and bowed on purpose while another has grown this way, so the character of wild animals is corrupt not on account of bad habits, but by nature. As for infants, nature impels them, not to seek pleasure, but simply to love themselves, to want to be safe and sound. Every living being, as soon as it is born, loves itself and all its parts, and especially cherishes the two most important ones, its mind and its body, and then their parts. And there are certain significant properties both of the mind and of the body of which it first has a vague intuition

[34] In his primis naturalibus voluptas insit necne, magna quaestio est. Nihil vero putare esse praeter voluptatem, non membra, non sensus, non ingenii motum, non integritatem corporis, non valitudinem, summae mihi videtur inscitiae. Atque ab isto capite fluere necesse est omnem rationem bonorum et malorum.

(. . .)

[36] Nam quod ait sensibus ipsis iudicari voluptatem bonum esse, dolorem malum, plus tribuit sensibus quam nobis leges permittunt, cum privatarum litium iudices sumus. Nihil enim possumus iudicare nisi quod est nostri iudicii. In quo frustra iudices solent, cum sententiam pronuntiant, addere, “si quid mei iudicii est”; si enim non fuit

and that it then begins to discern more clearly, with the result that it pursues these first gifts of nature and avoids their opposites.

[34] Whether pleasure is one of these "first things according to nature"[11] is a controversial question. But to claim that it's only pleasure—not one's limbs, sense perception, mental activity, soundness of body, or health—that seems to me completely stupid. Anyway, it's from this source that all discussion of good and evil must take its start.

(. . .)

[36] When Epicurus claims that the senses themselves judge pleasure to be a good thing and pain to be a bad one, he grants more power to the senses than the laws give to us when we are sitting on a jury in a civil trial. For there we can't make judgments on anything except on what is at issue in the trial. Which is why it's redundant

eorum iudicii, nihilo magis hoc non addito illud est iudicatum. Quid iudicant sensus? Dulce amarum, leve asperum, prope longe, stare movere, quadratum rotundum.

[37] Aequam igitur pronuntiabit sententiam ratio adhibita primum divinarum humanarumque rerum scientia, quae potest appellari rite sapientia, deinde adiunctis virtutibus, quas ratio rerum omnium dominas, tu voluptatum satellites et ministras esse voluisti. Quarum adeo omnium sententia pronuntiabit primum de voluptate, nihil esse ei loci non modo ut sola ponatur in summi boni sede quam quaerimus, sed ne illo quidem modo, ut ad honestatem applicetur. De vacuitate doloris eadem sententia erit.

for jurors, when they give their verdict, to add the formula "if it falls within my jurisdiction"; if it isn't within their jurisdiction, they can't make a judgment, whether they add the formula or not.[12] What is the jurisdiction of the senses? Sweet and bitter, smooth and rough, close and far, rest and movement, square and round.

[37] Therefore it is reason that will pronounce a sound judgment, applying first its knowledge of human and divine matters, which may rightly be called wisdom, and then making use of the virtues, which reason considers the mistresses of all things, but which you want to be the attendants and servants of the pleasures. And following their unanimous opinion, reason will pronounce the following verdict: there is no room for pleasure; not only does it not on its own take its place as the greatest good, which is what we are looking for, but it won't even do so

[38] Reicietur etiam Carneades, nec ulla de summo bono ratio aut voluptatis non dolendive particeps aut honestatis expers probabitur. Ita relinquet duas, de quibus etiam atque etiam consideret. Aut enim statuet nihil esse bonum nisi honestum, nihil malum nisi turpe, cetera aut omnino nihil habere momenti aut tantum ut nec expetenda nec fugienda, sed eligenda modo aut reicienda sint, aut anteponet eam quam cum honestate ornatissimam, tum etiam ipsis initiis naturae et totius perfectione vitae locupletatam videbit. Quod eo liquidius faciet, si perspexerit rerum inter eas verborumne sit controversia.

(. . .)

if you combine it with the morally good. And the verdict is going to be the same for freedom from pain.

[38] Reason will also reject the opinion of Carneades,[13] and will not approve of any theory of the greatest good that includes pleasure and pain or doesn't include the morally good. This leaves two theories, which reason will keep going over again and again. Either it will decide that nothing is good except virtue, and nothing bad except vice, while all other things have no significance or only so much that they're worthy of choice or rejection, but not of pursuit or avoidance. Or otherwise, it will prefer the theory that is not only splendid in morality but also enriched by the gifts of nature and a fulfilled life. And reason will come to its conclusion more easily once it has determined whether these two

[82] Illa videamus quae a te de amicitia dicta sunt. E quibus unum mihi videbar ab ipso Epicuro dictum cognoscere, amicitiam a voluptate non posse divelli ob eamque rem colendam esse quod, cum sine ea tuto et sine metu vivi non posset, ne iucunde quidem posset. Satis est ad hoc responsum. Attulisti aliud humanius horum recentiorum, numquam dictum ab ipso illo, quod sciam, primo utilitatis causa amicum expeti, cum autem usus accessisset, tum ipsum amari per se etiam omissa spe voluptatis. hoc etsi multimodis reprehendi potest, tamen accipio quod dant. Mihi enim satis est, ipsis non satis. Nam aliquando posse recte fieri dicunt nulla expectata nec quaesita voluptate.

theories are at variance in terms of content or only over words.[14]

(. . .)

[82] Let's look at what you said about friendship. There I seemed to recognize a saying of Epicurus, that friendship cannot be divorced from pleasure and that one needs to cultivate it for the reason that without it, one can't live safely and without fear, and not even pleasurably. About this sort of thing, I've said enough. You also mentioned a more humane version by those more recent Epicureans, something that was never put forth by Epicurus himself, as far as I know: we first seek friends for their usefulness, but once we have grown close to them, we love them for their own sakes even if there is no chance of gaining pleasure. One could criticize this in various ways, but I'll accept what they have to offer. It's good enough for me, but it's

[83] Posuisti etiam dicere alios foedus quoddam inter se facere sapientis, ut, quem ad modum sint in se ipsos animati, eodem modo sint erga amicos; id et fieri posse et saepe esse factum et ad voluptates percipiendas maxime pertinere. Hoc foedus facere si potuerunt, faciant etiam illud, ut aequitatem modestiam virtutes omnes per se ipsas gratis diligant. An vero, si fructibus et emolumentis et utilitatibus amicitias colemus, si nulla caritas erit quae faciat amicitiam ipsam sua sponte, vi sua, ex se et propter se expetendam, dubium est quin fundos et insulas amicis anteponamus?

not good enough for them. For this way they are saying that sometimes moral action takes place without the expectation or purpose of pleasure.

[83] You also claimed that the wise make a kind of pact among themselves, to take the same attitude toward their friends that they have toward themselves; this, you said, is possible, happens often, and is very useful for gaining pleasures. If they can make this kind of pact, let them also make another one—namely, to love fairness, propriety, and all the virtues for their own sakes, without an expectation of reward. But really, if we cultivate friendships for gain, profit, and utility, and if there is no affection that by its own force spontaneously renders friendship desirable for itself, can there be any doubt that we shouldn't prefer our land holdings and urban real estate to our friends?

[84] Licet hic rursus ea commemores quae optimis verbis ab Epicuro de laude amicitiae dicta sunt. Non quaero quid dicat, sed quid convenienter possit rationi et sententiae suae dicere. "Utilitatis causa amicitia est quaesita." Num igitur utiliorem tibi hunc Triarium putas esse posse quam si tua sint Puteolis granaria? Collige omnia quae soletis: "Praesidium amicorum." Satis est tibi in te, satis in legibus, satis in mediocribus amicitiis praesidii. Iam contemni non poteris; odium autem et invidiam facile vitabis. Ad eas enim res ab Epicuro praecepta dantur. Et tamen tantis vectigalibus ad liberalitatem utens etiam sine hac Pyladea amicitia multorum te benivolentia praeclare tuebere et munies.

[85] "At quicum ioca seria, ut dicitur, quicum arcana, quicum occulta omnia?" Tecum optime, deinde etiam cum mediocri amico. sed fac ista esse

[84] Here you might again cite at me Epicurus's well-phrased sayings in praise of friendship. I don't want to know what he says, but what can be said that agrees with his doctrine and reasoning. "Friendship is sought for its usefulness." Do you really think Triarius here can be more useful to you than your granaries in Puteoli[15]? Muster all your usual arguments: "Friends offer protection." You have enough protection in yourself, in the laws, in ordinary acquaintanceships. You are in a position to be taken seriously, and you'll easily avoid hatred and envy. Epicurus can give you tips for that. And if you use your assets in a generous way, you will guard and protect yourself through the good will of many, even without that Pyladean friendship.[16]

[85] "But with whom can I share jokes and serious matters, as they say, with whom my innermost secrets?" Easily with yourself, or also

non inportuna: quid ad utilitatem tantae pecuniae? Vides igitur, si amicitiam sua caritate metiare, nihil esse praestantius, sin emolumento, summas familiaritates praediorum fructuosorum mercede superari. Me igitur ipsum ames oportet, non mea, si veri amici futuri sumus. Sed in rebus apertissimis nimium longi sumus. Perfecto enim et concluso neque virtutibus neque amicitiis usquam locum esse si ad voluptatem omnia referantur, nihil praeterea est magnopere dicendum.

(. . .)

[118] Ac ne plura complectar (sunt enim innumerabilia), bene laudata virtus voluptatis aditus intercludat necesse est. Quod iam a me expectare noli: tute introspice in mentem tuam ipse eamque omni cogitatione pertractans percontare ipse te perpetuisne malis voluptatibus perfruens in ea quam

with any old acquaintance. But even if that sort of thing is nice, how does it stack up against the usefulness of great wealth? There you see that if you judge friendship by affection, nothing is more outstanding; if you judge it by usefulness, the greatest friendships are surpassed by the profit of fertile fields. So if we are going to be true friends, you need to love *me*, not my possessions. But I am belaboring the obvious. The long and short of it is that if everything aims at pleasure, then there is no room for either virtues or friends; there is nothing much left to say.

(. . .)

[118] And not to keep going on (though I could do so forever): once virtue has been justly extolled, it by necessity closes off the path to pleasure. Don't ask me to do this job: look into your own mind, examine it long and hard, and ask yourself if you really prefer to spend your

saepe usurpabas tranquillitate degere omnem aetatem sine dolore, adsumpto etiam illo quod vos quidem adiungere soletis sed fieri non potest, sine doloris metu, an, cum de omnibus gentibus optime mererere, cum opem indigentibus salutemque ferres, vel Herculis perpeti aerumnas. Sic enim maiores nostri labores non fugiendos tristissimo tamen verbo aerumnas etiam in deo nominaverunt. [119] Elicerem ex te cogeremque ut responderes, nisi vererer ne Herculem ipsum ea quae pro salute gentium summo labore gessisset voluptatis causa gessisse diceres.

whole life enjoying perpetual pleasures in your much-vaunted tranquility without pain and, as you like to add (though that's not really possible), even without fear of pain. Or would you prefer to undergo even the labors of Hercules as long as you can do good to the world and bring help and salvation to those in need? Even though he was a god, this is what our ancestors called the toils he chose to undergo, with that off-putting word: labors. [119] I would twist and force a response out of you, if I weren't afraid that you will claim that when Hercules toiled for the salvation of mankind, he did so for the sake of pleasure!

[1] Voluptatem quidem, Brute, si ipsa pro se loquatur nec tam pertinaces habeat patronos, concessuram arbitror convictam superiore libro dignitati. Etenim sit inpudens, si virtuti diutius repugnet aut si honestis iucunda anteponat aut pluris esse contendat dulcedinem corporis ex eave natam laetitiam quam gravitatem animi atque constantiam. Quare illam quidem dimittamus et suis se finibus tenere iubeamus, ne blanditiis eius inlecebrisque impediatur disputandi severitas.

BOOK 3

The Virtues of Stoicism

Cicero addresses Brutus, the work's dedicatee.[1]

[1] I believe, Brutus, that if Pleasure could speak for herself and didn't have such persistent champions, she would yield to Worthiness, having been defeated in the previous book. She would be really shameless if she continued to compete with Virtue, put what's delightful above what's moral, or claim that sweet physical sensations and the joy that arises from them are worth more than dignity and constancy of mind. Therefore let's send her packing and tell her to keep within her

[2] quaerendum est enim ubi sit illud summum bonum quod reperire volumus, quoniam et voluptas ab eo remota est et eadem fere contra eos dici possunt qui vacuitatem doloris finem bonorum esse voluerunt. Nec vero ullum probetur summum bonum quod virtute careat, qua nihil potest esse praestantius.

Itaque quamquam in eo sermone qui cum Torquato est habitus non remissi fuimus, tamen haec acrior est cum Stoicis parata contentio. Quae enim de voluptate dicuntur, ea nec acutissime nec abscondite disseruntur; neque enim qui defendunt eam versuti in disserendo sunt nec qui contra dicunt causam difficilem refellunt.

(. . .)

own boundaries and not to hinder our serious inquiry with her charming enticements.

[2] For we must investigate where the greatest good that we are trying to find is situated, given that pleasure has nothing to do with it, and pretty much the same argument can be made against those who claim that the greatest good is freedom from pain. And let's not approve any theory of the greatest good that doesn't include virtue, for nothing can be put above it.

I wasn't a slouch in the conversation I had with Torquatus, but my upcoming battle with the Stoics is going to be tougher. Arguments about pleasure aren't particularly sophisticated or recondite. Those who make its case aren't well versed in debate, and those who oppose it don't find it hard to refute them.

(. . .)

[16] Placet his, inquit, quorum ratio mihi probatur, simul atque natum sit animal (hinc enim est ordiendum), ipsum sibi conciliari et commendari ad se conservandum et ad suum statum eaque quae conservantia sint eius status diligenda, alienari autem ab interitu iisque rebus quae interitum videantur adferre. Id ita esse sic probant, quod antequam voluptas aut dolor attigerit, salutaria appetant parvi aspernenturque contraria, quod non fieret nisi statum suum diligerent, interitum timerent. Fieri autem non posset ut appeterent aliquid nisi sensum haberent sui eoque se diligerent. Ex quo intellegi debet principium ductum esse a se diligendo.

In conversation with Cicero, Cato explains the Stoic view.[2]

[16] The philosophers with whose teaching I agree hold the following: as soon as a living creature is born (for that's where we have to start), it becomes attached to itself and concerned with its own preservation. It loves its own condition and what keeps up this condition, and shrinks from destruction and what appears to threaten destruction. And their proof for this is that even before pleasure or pain affects them, babies seek out what is beneficial to them and avoid the opposite, which they wouldn't do if they didn't love their own condition and were afraid of its destruction. And they wouldn't be able to seek out anything if they didn't have an awareness of themselves and thus loved themselves. And so we see that self-love is the first motivation.

[17] In principiis autem naturalibus plerique Stoici non putant voluptatem esse ponendam. Quibus ego vehementer assentior ne, si voluptatem natura posuisse in iis rebus videatur quae primae appetuntur, multa turpia sequantur. Satis esse autem argumenti videtur quam ob rem illa quae prima sunt adscita natura diligamus, quod est nemo quin, cum utrumvis liceat, aptas malit et integras omnis partis corporis quam, eodem usu, imminutas aut detortas habere.

Rerum autem cognitiones, quas vel comprehensiones vel perceptiones vel, si haec verba aut minus placent aut minus intelleguntur, catalepsis appellemus licet, eas igitur ipsas propter se adsciscendas arbitramur, quod habeant quiddam in se quasi complexum et continens veritatem. Id autem in parvis intellegi potest, quos delectari videamus,

[17] Most Stoics don't think that pleasure should be reckoned among the primary natural motivations. I strongly agree with this: if we thought that nature had placed pleasure among those things that we seek out first and foremost, there would be many shameful consequences. And the love that we feel for what nature first makes us pursue is sufficiently proved by the fact that there are no people who, given the choice, wouldn't rather have all parts of their bodies be sound and shapely, as opposed to stunted or twisted, even if their use were unimpaired.

We believe that cognition (we might also say grasping or perception or—if these words aren't appealing or easily comprehensible—*katalēpsis*) should be sought for its own sake, because it contains something that, as it were, embraces and holds on to the truth. You can observe this in small children, who are delighted when they have

etiamsi eorum nihil intersit, si quid ratione per se ipsi invenerint. [18] Artis etiam ipsas propter se assumendas putamus, cum quia sit in iis aliquid dignum assumptione, tum quod constent ex cognitionibus et contineant quiddam in se ratione constitutum et via. A falsa autem assensione magis nos alienatos esse quam a ceteris rebus quae sint contra naturam arbitrantur.

(. . .)

[19] Haec dicuntur fortasse ieiunius; sunt enim quasi prima elementa naturae, quibus ubertas orationis adhiberi vix potest, nec equidem eam cogito consectari. Verum tamen cum de rebus grandioribus dicas, ipsae res verba rapiunt; ita fit cum gravior, tum etiam splendidior oratio.

figured something out by their own reasoning, even if it makes no difference to them. [18] And we think that the arts and sciences should be pursued for their own sakes, not only because they're themselves worthy of pursuit, but also because they're based on cognition and contain the product of some kind of rational method. And the Stoics believe that assenting to false propositions is more alien to our nature than all other things that are contrary to nature.

(. . .)

[19] These matters are perhaps a bit dry. They are, so to speak, the basics of nature, which hardly allow for rhetorical flourishes, and so I'm not aiming at that. But when one speaks of greater things, then the subject itself moves one's words along, and one's speech becomes more splendid the more serious it is.

Est ut dicis, inquam. Sed tamen omne, quod de re bona dilucide dicitur mihi praeclare dici videtur. Istius modi autem res dicere ornate velle puerile est, plane autem et perspicue expedire posse docti et intellegentis viri.

[20] Progrediamur igitur quoniam, inquit, ab his principiis naturae discessimus quibus congruere debent quae sequuntur. Sequitur autem haec prima divisio: aestimabile esse dicunt (sic enim, ut opinor, appellemus) id quod aut ipsum secundum naturam sit aut tale quid efficiat, ut selectione dignum propterea sit quod aliquod pondus habeat dignum aestimatione, quam illi ἀξίαν vocant, contraque inaestimabile quod sit superiori contrarium. Initiis igitur ita constitutis ut ea quae secundum naturam sunt ipsa propter se sumenda sint contrariaque item reicienda, primum est officium (id enim appello καθῆκον) ut se conservet in

Very true, I said. But I believe that everything that is said clearly about a worthy topic is well said. It's childish to attempt to speak about matters of this kind in an elaborate manner, and a learned and intelligent person will simply explain them in easily comprehensible language.

[20] So let's go on, he said, since we have digressed from those primary natural motivations that must form the basis of everything that follows. What comes next is this first distinction: the Stoics call "valuable" (I think that's the term we should use) whatever is either itself according to nature or produces something that is. It's worthy of choice because it contains something of significant value (what the Stoics call *axia*); the opposite of this is "nonvaluable." The basic principle is thus that what is according to nature should be pursued for its own sake and what is the opposite should be rejected. "Appropriate

naturae statu, deinceps ut ea teneat quae secundum naturam sint pellatque contraria. Qua inventa selectione et item reiectione sequitur deinceps cum officio selectio, deinde ea perpetua, tum ad extremum constans consentaneaque naturae, in qua primum inesse incipit et intellegi quid sit quod vere bonum possit dici.

[21] Prima est enim conciliatio hominis ad ea quae sunt secundum naturam. Simul autem cepit intellegentiam vel notionem potius (quam appellant ἔννοιαν illi) viditque rerum agendarum ordinem et, ut ita dicam, concordiam, multo eam pluris aestimavit quam omnia illa quae prima dilexerat, atque ita cognitione et ratione collegit ut statueret in eo collocatum summum illud hominis per se laudandum et expetendum bonum.

action" (that's my translation of *kathēkon*) is, first, to preserve oneself in one's natural state and, second, to hold on to what is according to nature and push away the opposite. Once this principle of selection and rejection has been established, appropriate action means making choices, which then become a habit and finally a consistent process in accordance with nature. And this is where what can truly be called good begins to show itself and to be understood.

[21] The attachment of human beings to what is according to nature is only the first step. As soon as we develop intelligence or rather insight (what the Stoics call *ennoia*), and understand the principles or, so to speak, coherence of appropriate actions, we value that much higher than all the things we loved at first. And with the help of cognition and reason, we come to understand that this is where the greatest human good is

Quod cum positum sit in eo quod ὁμολογίαν Stoici, nos appellemus convenientiam, si placet—cum igitur in eo sit id bonum quo omnia referenda sint, honeste facta ipsumque honestum—quod solum in bonis ducitur, quamquam post oritur—tamen id solum vi sua et dignitate expetendum est; eorum autem, quae sunt prima naturae, propter se nihil est expetendum.

[22] Cum vero illa quae officia esse dixi proficiscantur ab initiis naturae, necesse est ea ad haec referri, ut recte dici possit omnia officia eo referri ut adipiscamur principia naturae, nec tamen ut hoc sit bonorum ultimum, propterea quod non inest in primis naturae conciliationibus honesta actio; consequens enim est et post oritur, ut dixi. Est tamen

located, the one that is praise- and choiceworthy in its own right. It's placed in what the Stoics called *homologia* and what we'll call consistency, if you don't mind. That is where that good lies to which all other things need to be directed: it is moral action and morality itself. This is the only thing that counts as a good; it arises later but nevertheless is the only thing to be pursued on account of its own character and value. By contrast, none of the first things according to nature is worthy of being pursued in and of itself.

[22] Since the appropriate actions I have mentioned arise from the primary natural concerns, they must by necessity be directed at them, so that we can rightly say that all appropriate actions aim at acquiring the first things according to nature. But that doesn't mean that this is the greatest good: moral action doesn't belong to

ea secundum naturam multoque nos ad se expetendam magis hortatur quam superiora omnia.

Sed ex hoc primum error tollendus est, ne quis sequi existimet ut duo sint ultima bonorum. Ut enim si cui propositum sit conliniare hastam aliquo aut sagittam, sic nos ultimum in bonis dicimus. Huic in eiusmodi similitudine omnia sint facienda ut conliniet, et tamen, ut omnia faciat quo propositum adsequatur, sit hoc quasi ultimum (quale nos summum in vita bonum dicimus), illud autem, ut feriat, quasi seligendum, non expetendum.

[23] Cum autem omnia officia a principiis naturae proficiscantur, ab isdem necesse est proficisci ipsam sapientiam. Sed quem ad modum saepe fit ut is qui commendatus sit alicui pluris eum faciat

the natural attachments; as I have explained, it arises only later. It is nevertheless according to nature and inspires us to embrace itself much more than all the earlier things do.[3]

But here we first have to guard against a misunderstanding, so that no one gets the idea that there are therefore two greatest goods. We maintain that with the final good, it's as when a man is attempting to aim a spear or an arrow at some target. The point of comparison is this: he needs to do everything to aim straight, and his final purpose (the equivalent of what in life we call the greatest good) is to give his all in doing so. But to *hit* the target, that's, as it were, an outcome to be selected, but not to be sought.[4]

[23] And since all appropriate actions take their start from the primary natural motivations, wisdom must take its start from them as well. But just as it often happens that, when we have

cui commendatus sit quam illum a quo, sic minime mirum est primo nos sapientiae commendari ab initiis naturae, post autem ipsam sapientiam nobis cariorem fieri quam illa sint a quibus ad hanc venerimus. Atque ut membra nobis ita data sunt ut ad quandam rationem vivendi data esse appareant, sic appetitio animi, quae ὁρμή Graece vocatur, non ad quodvis genus vitae sed ad quandam formam vivendi videtur data, itemque et ratio et perfecta ratio.

[24] Ut enim histrioni actio, saltatori motus non quivis sed certus quidam est datus, sic vita agenda est certo genere quodam, non quolibet; quod genus conveniens consentaneumque dicimus. Nec enim gubernationi aut medicinae similem sapientiam esse arbitramur, sed actioni illi potius quam

been introduced to a person by someone else, we end up preferring our new acquaintance to the person who introduced us, so it is not surprising that we are first introduced to wisdom by the primary natural motivations, but then hold wisdom much dearer than the things that led us to her. And just as our limbs appear to have been given to us for the purpose of a certain manner of living, so our mind's desire (called *hormē* in Greek) seems to have been given to us not for any random type of life, but for a specific form of living; and the same is true for reason and right reason.

[24] And just as an actor has been given a role, and a dancer a movement, that isn't random but well-defined, so life must be lived not in any old way, but in a specific fashion—a fashion that we call fitting and appropriate. For we don't think that wisdom is similar to navigation or medicine,

modo dixi et saltationi, ut in ipsa insit, non foris petatur extremum, id est artis effectio. Et tamen est etiam aliqua cum his ipsis artibus sapientiae dissimilitudo, propterea quod in illis quae recte facta sunt non continent tamen omnes partes e quibus constant. Quae autem nos aut recta aut recte facta dicamus, si placet, illi autem appellant κατορθώματα, omnes numeros virtutis continent. Sola enim sapientia in se tota conversa est, quod idem in ceteris artibus non fit.

[25] Inscite autem medicinae et gubernationis ultimum cum ultimo sapientiae comparatur. Sapientia enim et animi magnitudinem complectitur et iustitiam et ut omnia quae homini accidant infra se esse iudicet, quod idem ceteris artibus non contingit. Tenere autem virtutes eas ipsas quarum modo feci mentionem nemo poterit nisi statuerit

but rather, as I've just said, to acting and dancing: there the final purpose, the realization of the art, is inherent in its practice and not something external. There is, however, also a difference between wisdom and these arts. Any instance of their correct execution doesn't involve all their constituent parts at the same time. By contrast, what we shall, if you like, call correct or correctly executed actions (the Stoics call them *katorthōmata*) contain all elements of virtue. Only wisdom is entirely directed at itself, something that doesn't happen with the other arts.

[25] By contrast, to compare the purpose of medicine and navigation with the final good of wisdom makes no sense. Wisdom also comprises greatness of spirit, justice, and the belief that it is above anything that can befall human beings; that's not true of the other arts. And no one can attain those virtues I have just mentioned unless

nihil esse quod intersit aut differat aliud ab alio praeter honesta et turpia.

[26] Videamus nunc quam sint praeclare illa his quae iam posui consequentia. Cum enim hoc sit extremum (sentis enim, credo, me iam diu quod τέλος Graeci dicant id dicere tum extremum, tum ultimum, tum summum; licebit etiam finem pro extremo aut ultimo dicere)—cum igitur hoc sit extremum, congruenter naturae convenienterque vivere, necessario sequitur omnes sapientes semper feliciter absolute fortunate vivere, nulla re impediri, nulla prohiberi, nulla egere.
(. . .)

[29] Quid vero? Negarine ullo modo possit numquam quemquam stabili et firmo et magno

they first hold that there is nothing that makes any difference or distinguishes one thing from another except what is moral and what is shameful.

[26] Let us now consider the excellent consequences of what I have been talking about. Since this is the final good (I think you will have noticed that what the Greeks call the *telos*, I sometimes call the "final," sometimes the "last," sometimes the "greatest"; instead of the "final" and "last," we can also call it the "end")—since this is thus the final good, to live in accordance and in harmony with nature, it follows necessarily that all wise people live forever in perfect bliss and happiness, without any impediment, hindrance, or want.

(. . .)

[29] Therefore what? Can it be at all denied that there can never be a person of a stable, steadfast,

animo, quem fortem virum dicimus, effici posse, nisi constitutum sit non esse malum dolorem? Ut enim qui mortem in malis ponit non potest eam non timere, sic nemo ulla in re potest id quod malum esse decreverit non curare idque contemnere. Quo posito et omnium adsensu approbato illud adsumitur, eum qui magno sit animo atque forti omnia quae cadere in hominem possint despicere ac pro nihilo putare. Quae cum ita sint, effectum est nihil esse malum quod turpe non sit. Atque iste vir altus et excellens, magno animo, vere fortis, infra se omnia humana ducens, is, inquam, quem efficere volumus, quem quaerimus, certe et confidere sibi debet ac suae vitae et actae et consequenti et bene de sese iudicare, statuens nihil posse mali incidere sapienti. Ex quo intellegitur idem illud, solum bonum esse quod honestum sit, idque esse beate vivere: honeste—id est cum virtute—vivere. (. . .)

and spirited disposition, the type we call brave, if it hasn't been established that pain is not an evil? Just as a person who considers death an evil cannot avoid being afraid of it, so in no way can someone who has decided that something is an evil not worry about it and simply dismiss it. Everybody can agree on this, and once this has been established, it follows that the great-hearted and brave person looks down on all things that can befall human beings and considers them of no account. And thus we come to the conclusion that there is no evil except vice. Those lofty and outstanding persons, great-hearted, truly brave, considering all human vicissitudes beneath them, the very ones we are looking for and wish to create—they certainly must have confidence in themselves and in their own lives, both past and future, and judge well of themselves, convinced that nothing bad can

[41] Tum ille, his igitur ita positis, inquit, sequitur magna contentio, quam tractatam a Peripateticis mollius (est enim eorum consuetudo dicendi non satis acuta propter ignorationem dialecticae) Carneades tuus egregia quadam exercitatione in dialecticis summaque eloquentia rem in summum discrimen adduxit, propterea quod pugnare non destitit in omni hac quaestione quae de bonis et malis appelletur non esse rerum Stoicis cum Peripateticis controversiam sed nominum. Mihi autem nihil tam perspicuum videtur quam has sententias eorum philosophorum re inter se magis quam verbis dissidere. Maiorem multo inter Stoicos et Peripateticos rerum esse aio discrepantiam quam

happen to a wise person. And so we see that what is morally good is the only good, and that that's what the happy life is: to live morally—that is, with virtue.

(. . .)

[41] Then Cato said, now that we have established this, we come to a great controversy. The Peripatetics approached the matter in a somewhat subdued fashion (their style of argument was less stringent than usual because they didn't know dialectic). Your Carneades, by contrast, who had some very good training in dialectic and was extremely eloquent, made it a major bone of contention, especially since he never backed off from his provocative assertion that, in this whole so-called question of good and evil the controversy between Stoics and the Peripatetics isn't over substance but only over terminology.[5] But to me, nothing seems clearer than

verborum, quippe cum Peripatetici omnia quae ipsi bona appellant pertinere dicant ad beate vivendum, nostri non ex omni quod aestimatione aliqua dignum sit, compleri vitam beatam putent.

[42] An vero certius quicquam potest esse quam illorum ratione qui dolorem in malis ponunt non posse sapientem beatum esse cum eculeo torqueatur? Eorum autem qui dolorem in malis non habent ratio certe cogit ut in omnibus tormentis conservetur beata vita sapienti. Etenim si dolores eosdem tolerabilius patiuntur qui excipiunt eos pro patria quam qui leviore de causa, opinio facit, non natura, vim doloris aut maiorem aut minorem.

that the doctrines of these philosophers are different in content more than in form. I maintain that between the Stoics and the Peripatetics there is far greater disagreement in substance than in terminology: the Peripatetics claim that all the things they call goods contribute to the happy life, while for us Stoics, not everything we consider to be of value is also needed for a completely happy life.

[42] But can there be anything more obvious than the fact that, by the Peripatetic reasoning, which counts pain as an evil, the wise person cannot be happy when tortured on the rack? But the reasoning of those who do not consider pain an evil clearly secures the wise person's happiness even under torture. If it's the case that those who undergo pain in service of the fatherland tolerate it more easily than those who undergo the same amount of pain for a more trivial reason,

[43] Ne illud quidem est consentaneum ut si, cum tria genera bonorum sint, quae sententia est Peripateticorum, eo beatior quisque sit quo sit corporis aut externis bonis plenior, ut hoc idem approbandum sit nobis ut qui plura habeat ea quae in corpore magni aestimantur sit beatior. Illi enim corporis commodis compleri vitam beatam putant, nostri nihil minus. Nam cum ita placeat, ne eorum quidem bonorum quae nos bona vere appellemus frequentia beatiorem vitam fieri aut magis expetendam aut pluris aestimandam, certe minus ad beatam vitam pertinet multitudo corporis commodorum.

[44] Etenim si et sapere expetendum sit et valere, coniunctum utrumque magis expetendum

then it is attitude, not nature, that renders pain more or less intense.

[43] And we also don't agree with the idea that, if there are three kinds of goods (which is what the Peripatetics think), people are the happier the more they're supplied with bodily and external goods.[6] That way we would also have to agree that people are happier if they have more of those physical attributes that are supposed to be of great value. For the Peripatetics believe that the happy life is made complete by physical advantages, but the Stoics don't think so at all. Even in the case of those goods that we truly consider goods, we don't think that it's their quantity that makes a life happier, more desirable, or more valuable; so surely a multitude of bodily advantages has even less impact on the happy life.

[44] If both wisdom and health are worthy of being sought as goods, then both of them in

sit quam sapere solum, neque tamen, si utrumque sit aestimatione dignum, pluris sit coniunctum quam sapere ipsum separatim. Nam qui valitudinem aestimatione aliqua dignam iudicamus neque eam tamen in bonis ponimus, idem censemus nullam esse tantam aestimationem, ut ea virtuti anteponatur. Quod idem Peripatetici non tenent, quibus dicendum est quae et honesta actio sit et sine dolore eam magis esse expetendam quam si esset eadem actio cum dolore. Nobis aliter videtur, recte secusne, postea; sed potestne rerum maior esse dissensio?

[45] Ut enim obscuratur et offunditur luce solis lumen lucernae, et ut interit in magnitudine maris Aegaei stilla mellis, et ut in divitiis Croesi terunci accessio et gradus unus in ea via quae est hinc in Indiam, sic, cum sit is bonorum finis quem Stoici

combination are more desirable than just wisdom on its own. However, if both are considered to be simply of value, then this doesn't mean that their combination is worth more than wisdom on its own. We believe that health has a certain value, but we don't think it's a good, and we also believe that there is nothing so valuable as to surpass virtue. The Peripatetics don't agree, and therefore they have to maintain that one should choose a moral action not accompanied by pain over the same action with pain. We don't think so—whether rightly or wrongly, we shall see. But could there be a greater disagreement in terms of substance?

[45] The light of a lamp is eclipsed and obscured by sunlight; a drop of honey gets lost in the vastness of the Aegean Sea; and an extra penny makes no difference to the riches of Croesus,[7] just as one single step doesn't shorten the

dicunt, omnis ista rerum corporearum aestimatio splendore virtutis et magnitudine obscuretur et obruatur atque intereat necesse est. Et quem ad modum opportunitas (sic enim appellemus εὐκαιρίαν) non fit maior productione temporis (habent enim suum modum quae opportuna dicuntur), sic recta effectio (κατόρθωσιν enim ita appello, quoniam rectum factum κατόρθωμα)—recta igitur effectio, item convenientia, denique ipsum bonum, quod in eo positum est ut naturae consentiat, crescendi accessionem nullam habet. (. . .)

[50] Deinceps explicatur differentia rerum, quam si non ullam esse diceremus, confunderetur omnis vita, ut ab Aristone, neque ullum sapientiae munus aut opus inveniretur, cum inter res eas quae ad vitam degendam pertinerent nihil omnino interesset neque ullum dilectum adhiberi oporteret.

journey from here to India. In the same way, if the Stoics are right about the greatest good, all those valuable bodily attributes are by necessity eclipsed, swept away, and annihilated by the splendor and magnitude of virtue. And just as good timing (that'll be our translation of *eukaria*) doesn't become better with the passage of time (for good timing is of limited duration), so correct behavior (that's my word for *katorthōsis*, since *katorthōma* is correct action), consistency, and the good itself (which consists in accordance with nature) cannot be increased.

(. . .)

[50] And now I will explain how things differ from one another. If we didn't think they did, life would be thrown into complete confusion, as with Aristo, and there wouldn't be any job or task left for wisdom if there were no difference whatsoever among those things that are relevant

Itaque cum esset satis constitutum id solum esse bonum quod esset honestum et id malum solum quod turpe, tum inter illa quae nihil valerent ad beate misereve vivendum aliquid tamen quod differret esse voluerunt, ut essent eorum alia aestimabilia, alia contra, alia neutrum.

[51] Quae autem aestimanda essent, eorum in aliis satis esse causae quam ob rem quibusdam anteponerentur, ut in valitudine, ut in integritate sensuum, ut in doloris vacuitate, ut gloriae divitiarum similium rerum, alia autem non esse eiusmodi, itemque eorum quae nulla aestimatione digna essent partim satis habere causae quam ob rem reicerentur, ut dolorem morbum sensuum amissionem paupertatem ignominiam similia horum, partim non item.
(. . .)

for the conduct of life, and if there weren't a need for making choices. After having established that nothing is good except virtue and nothing bad except vice, the Stoics still want there to be a distinction among those things that do not contribute to living happily or unhappily: they hold that some are valuable, others nonvaluable, and others neither.[8]

[51] Some of the valuable things afford us adequate grounds for preferring them to others, such as health, unimpaired senses, freedom from pain, or glory, wealth, and the like; others don't. Likewise, some of the nonvaluable ones afford us adequate grounds for rejecting them, such as pain, illness, loss of sense perception, poverty, bad reputation, and the like; others don't.

(. . .)

[74] Sed iam sentio me esse longius provectum quam proposita ratio postularet. Verum admirabilis compositio disciplinae incredibilisque rerum me traxit ordo. Quem, per deos immortales, nonne miraris? Quid enim aut in natura, qua nihil est aptius, nihil descriptius, aut in operibus manu factis tam compositum tamque compactum et coagmentatum inveniri potest? Quid posterius priori non convenit? Quid sequitur quod non respondeat superiori? Quid non sic aliud ex alio nectitur ut, si unam litteram moveris, labent omnia? Nec tamen quicquam est quod moveri possit.

[75] Quam gravis vero, quam magnifica, quam constans conficitur persona sapientis! Qui, cum ratio docuerit, quod honestum esset id esse solum bonum, semper sit necesse est beatus vereque

[74] I'm aware that I have gone on for longer than necessary. But the amazing architecture of our system and the unbelievable arrangement of the subject matter have carried me away. By the immortal gods, isn't it a marvel? What can be found that is better structured, devised, and joined together, either in nature (than which nothing is more fittingly arranged) or among man-made objects? There is nothing that comes later that doesn't agree with what comes earlier, no conclusion that doesn't follow from its premise. Everything is so intrinsically connected to everything else that if you remove one single letter, the whole system collapses. In fact, there is nothing that can be removed!

[75] And the way the character of the wise has been conceived, how impressive, magnificent, and consistent! Since reason has taught the wise that virtue is the only good, they're by necessity

omnia ista nomina possideat quae irrideri ab inperitis solent. Rectius enim appellabitur rex quam Tarquinius, qui nec se nec suos regere potuit, rectius magister populi (is enim est dictator) quam Sulla, qui trium pestiferorum vitiorum, luxuriae avaritiae crudelitatis, magister fuit, rectius dives quam Crassus, qui nisi eguisset, numquam Euphraten nulla belli causa transire voluisset. Recte eius omnia dicentur qui scit uti solus omnibus, recte etiam pulcher appellabitur (animi enim liniamenta sunt pulchriora quam corporis), recte solus liber nec dominationi cuiusquam parens nec oboediens cupiditati, recte invictus, cuius etiamsi corpus constringatur, animo tamen vincula inici nulla possint.

always happy and rightfully lay claim to all those monikers that the clueless like to make fun of. The wise person is more rightly called "king" than Tarquin, who couldn't even rule himself or his own family members; more rightly "master of the people" (that is, dictator) than Sulla, who was the master of three pestilent vices, namely, luxury, avarice, and cruelty; and more rightly "rich" than Crassus, who wouldn't have decided to cross the Euphrates without any provocation to war if he hadn't been in want of something.[9] The wise are rightly said to own everything, since they alone understand how to make use of everything; they're rightly called beautiful, since the shape of the mind is more beautiful than the shape of the body; they alone are rightly called free and not subject to any master or in thrall to any desire; and rightly called invincible, since even if their bodies are restrained, their minds cannot be shackled.

[76] Nec expectet ullum tempus aetatis, uti tum denique iudicetur beatusne fuerit cum extremum vitae diem morte confecerit, quod ille unus e septem sapientibus non sapienter Croesum monuit. Nam si beatus umquam fuisset, beatam vitam usque ad illum a Cyro extructum rogum pertulisset. Quodsi ita est, ut neque quisquam nisi bonus vir et omnes boni beati sint, quid philosophia magis colendum aut quid est virtute divinius?

[76] Wise people do not have to wait for a particular time of their lives, so that on their dying day, it can finally be decided whether they have been happy or not—as was the unwise advice of one of the Seven Wise Men to Croesus. For if Croesus had ever been happy, he would have kept his happiness all the way onto that pyre built by Cyrus.[10] But since it is the case that no one is happy except the good person, and all good people are happy, what is more worthy of pursuit than philosophy, and what more divine than virtue?

[1] Quae cum dixisset, finem ille. Ego autem: Ne tu, inquam, Cato, ista exposuisti, ut tam multa memoriter, ut tam obscura dilucide. Itaque aut omittamus contra omnino velle aliquid aut spatium sumamus ad cogitandum; tam enim diligenter, etiam si minus vere (nam nondum id quidem audeo dicere), sed tamen accurate non modo fundatam, verum etiam exstructam disciplinam non est facile perdiscere.

Tum ille: Ain tandem? inquit, cum ego te hac nova lege videam eodem die accusatori respondere

BOOK 4

The Limits of a Stoic Life

Cicero challenges Cato's view.

[1] With these words, Cato concluded his speech. I said: Cato, you really have explained this enormous and obscure subject matter very accurately and clearly. I'll therefore either have to give up on responding altogether or I'll need some time to think about it. It's not easy to get a grip on a system that has been erected on such well-laid foundations with such great care—if perhaps not entirely in keeping with the truth (though I'm not yet prepared to say so).

He said: Are you serious? I have seen you respond to the prosecutor and then give a

et tribus horis perorare, in hac me causa tempus dilaturum putas? Quae tamen a te agetur non melior quam illae sunt quas interdum optines. Quare istam quoque aggredere, tractatam praesertim et ab aliis et a te ipso saepe, ut tibi deesse non possit oratio.

[2] Tum ego: Non mehercule, inquam, soleo temere contra Stoicos, non quo illis admodum assentiar, sed pudore impedior; ita multa dicunt, quae vix intellegam.

Obscura, inquit, quaedam esse confiteor, nec tamen ab illis ita dicuntur de industria, sed inest in rebus ipsis obscuritas.

Cur igitur easdem res, inquam, Peripateticis dicentibus verbum nullum est quod non intellegatur?

three-hour concluding speech, all on the same day, as per this new law.[1] So you think I'm going to grant you a deferral? And your case here is no better than the ones you sometimes take on. So go ahead and plead it—it's a subject that has been discussed by many and often by you as well, so you can't be at a loss for words.

[2] I said: Wait a moment! I don't go about rashly attacking the Stoics—not because I completely agree with them, but because I'm held back by embarrassment. They say so many things that I barely understand.

I admit that some of what they say is obscure, he said. But they don't talk this way on purpose, but because obscurity is inherent in the subject matter itself.

But when the Peripatetics say the same things, I said, why isn't there a single word that is incomprehensible?

Easdemne res? inquit. An parum disserui non verbis Stoicos a Peripateticis, sed universa re et tota sententia dissidere?

Atqui, inquam, Cato, si istud optinueris, traducas me ad te totum licebit.

Putabam equidem satis, inquit, me dixisse. Quare ad ea primum, si videtur; sin aliud quid voles, postea.

Immo istud quidem, inquam, quo loco quidque occurrerit, nisi iniquum postulo, arbitratu meo.

Ut placet, inquit. Etsi enim illud erat aptius, aequum cuique concedere.

[3] Existimo, igitur, inquam, Cato, veteres illos Platonis auditores, Speusippum, Aristotelem, Xenocratem, deinde eorum Polemonem, Theophrastum, satis et copiose et eleganter habuisse constitutam disciplinam, ut non esset causa Zenoni,

He said, the same things?! Haven't I been going on about how the Stoics and the Peripatetics disagree not in words but in substance, and as regards their entire doctrine?

I said, if you convince me of that, Cato, you can sign me up.

I really thought what I said was sufficient, said he. So if you like, let's talk about this first—or if you want to discuss something else first, we'll get to it later.

If you don't mind, I said, I'll treat each topic at my discretion, as it comes up.

Fine, he said. My approach would have been better, but to each his own.

[3] I said: I think, Cato, that those old students of Plato—Speusippus, Aristotle, and Xenocrates—as well their own students—Polemo and Theophrastus—had fully developed a detailed and sophisticated system of thought. So

cum Polemonem audisset, cur et ab eo ipso et a superioribus dissideret. Quorum fuit haec institutio, in qua animadvertas velim quid mutandum putes, nec expectes dum ad omnia dicam quae a te dicta sunt; universa enim illorum ratione cum tota vestra confligendum puto.

[4] Qui cum viderent ita nos esse natos ut et communiter ad eas virtutes apti essemus quae notae illustresque sunt, iustitiam dico, temperantiam, ceteras generis eiusdem (quae omnes similes artium reliquarum materia tantum ad meliorem partem et tractatione differunt), easque ipsas virtutes viderent nos magnificentius appetere et ardentius, habere etiam insitam quandam vel potius innatam cupiditatem scientiae natosque esse ad congregationem hominum et ad societatem

there was no reason why Zeno, who had studied with Polemo, should disagree with him or his predecessors.[2] Their system was the following—and please let me know immediately if you think something I say needs correction, and don't wait until I have responded to everything you have said. For I do think that their entire doctrine needs to be compared and contrasted with the entirety of yours.

[4] Those philosophers established the following: by nature, we all have a talent for those well-known and illustrious virtues—that is, justice, temperance, and the rest (these are all similar to the other arts, except that their subject matter and the way they treat it are superior). We strive for those virtues with remarkable eagerness and also have an innate desire for knowledge. We are further born to associate with other people and to pursue the society and community of the human

communitatemque generis humani, eaque in maximis ingeniis maxime elucere.

(. . .)

[14] Nunc videamus, quaeso, de summo bono, quod continet philosophiam, quid tandem attulerit, quam ob rem ab inventoribus tamquam a parentibus dissentiret. Hoc igitur loco, quamquam a te, Cato, diligenter est explicatum, finis hic bonorum et quis a Stoicis et quem ad modum diceretur, tamen ego quoque exponam, ut perspiciamus, si potuerimus, quidnam a Zenone novi sit allatum.

Cum enim superiores, e quibus planissime Polemo, secundum naturam vivere summum bonum esse dixissent, his verbis tria significari Stoici dicunt, unum eiusmodi, vivere adhibentem scientiam earum rerum quae natura evenirent. Hunc ipsum Zenonis aiunt esse finem declarantem illud

race. And these qualities are especially apparent in the most gifted people.

(. . .)

[14] So now, please, let's consider the greatest good, which is the foundation of philosophy. What innovations did Zeno make that led him to disagree with those earlier philosophers as if with his parents? You, Cato, have already given a careful exposition of what the Stoics say the greatest good is, and how they make their argument. Still, at this point, I want to lay it out myself, so that we can see, if possible, what Zeno added that was new.

The earlier philosophers, especially Polemo, said that the greatest good was living according to nature. The Stoics hold that this phrase can mean three things. First, to live by applying one's knowledge of the natural order of things. This, they say, is the greatest good according to

quod a te dictum est, convenienter naturae vivere. [15] Alterum significari idem ut si diceretur officia media omnia aut pleraque servantem vivere. Hoc sic expositum dissimile est superiori. Illud enim rectum est (quod κατόρθωμα dicebas) contingitque sapienti soli, hoc autem inchoati cuiusdam officii est, non perfecti, quod cadere in nonnullos insipientes potest.

Tertium autem omnibus aut maximis rebus iis quae secundum naturam sint fruentem vivere. Hoc non est positum in nostra actione; completur enim et ex eo genere vitae quod virtute fruitur et ex iis rebus quae sunt secundum naturam neque sunt in nostra potestate. Sed hoc summum bonum quod tertia significatione intellegitur, eaque vita quae ex summo bono degitur, quia coniuncta ei virtus est, in sapientem solum cadit, isque finis

Zeno himself, what you called "living in harmony with nature."[3] [15] The second meaning can be glossed as living by executing all appropriate actions or most of them. Put like this, it's different from the first definition. The first definition has to do with what is correct (what you called the *katorthōma*) and is open only to the wise. By contrast, the second definition concerns incomplete actions, not perfect ones, and may be open also to some nonwise people.

Last, the third meaning is living in the enjoyment of all, or the most important, things that are according to nature. This isn't up to us: it consists both of a mode of life that is based on virtue and on those things that are according to nature and aren't in our power. Even so, the greatest good as per this third definition, and the life led according to this greatest good, are open only to the wise, because virtue is part of them.

bonorum, ut ab ipsis Stoicis scriptum videmus, a Xenocrate atque ab Aristotele constitutus est. Itaque ab iis constitutio illa prima naturae, a qua tu quoque ordiebare, his prope verbis exponitur.

[16] Omnis natura vult esse conservatrix sui, ut et salva sit et in genere conservetur suo. Ad hanc rem aiunt artis quoque requisitas quae naturam adiuvarent, in quibus ea numeretur in primis quae est vivendi ars, ut tueatur quod a natura datum sit, quod desit adquirat. Idemque diviserunt naturam hominis in animum et corpus. Cumque eorum utrumque per se expetendum esse dixissent, virtutes quoque utriusque eorum per se expetendas esse dicebant; et cum animum infinita quadam laude anteponerent corpori, virtutes quoque animi bonis corporis anteponebant.

This, as the Stoics tell us themselves, is the greatest good posited by Xenocrates and Aristotle. And that basic argument about nature, from which you too started your discourse, was made by those two in the following fashion:

[16] every natural being wants to preserve itself, to be safe and to maintain itself as one of its kind. And they say that the arts were invented to assist nature, first and foremost what is called the art of life; it maintains what has been provided by nature and procures what is missing. They also divide human nature into mind and body. They say that each is valuable in its own right, and likewise that the virtues of each are valuable in their own right. But since they bestow nearly unlimited praise on the mind and rank it above the body, they also prefer the virtues of the mind to the goods of the body.

[17] Sed cum sapientiam totius hominis custodem et procuratricem esse vellent, quae esset naturae comes et adiutrix, hoc sapientiae munus esse dicebant ut, cum eum tueretur qui constaret ex animo et corpore, in utroque iuvaret eum ac contineret. Atque ita re simpliciter primo collocata reliqua subtilius persequentes corporis bona facilem quandam rationem habere censebant; de animi bonis accuratius exquirebant in primisque reperiebant inesse in iis iustitiae semina primique ex omnibus philosophis natura tributum esse docuerunt ut ii qui procreati essent a procreatoribus amarentur et, id quod temporum ordine antiquius est, ut coniugia virorum et uxorum natura coniuncta esse dicerent, qua ex stirpe orirentur amicitiae cognationum. Atque ab his initiis profecti omnium virtutum et originem et progressionem persecuti sunt. Ex quo magnitudo quoque animi exsistebat, qua facile posset repugnari

[17] They maintain that wisdom, which is the companion and helpmate of nature, is the guardian and caretaker of human beings in their entirety; accordingly, since wisdom takes care of creatures that consist of mind and body, it is its task to support and preserve them in respect of both. And having laid out this basic principle, those philosophers took a close look at its consequences. They thought the goods of the body were easy to understand, but examined the goods of the mind in greater detail. They concluded, first and foremost, that we carry in us the seeds of justice, and they were the first of all philosophers to maintain that it is natural for parents to love their offspring, that the union of husbands and wives (which comes earlier in time) is likewise motivated by nature, and that the affection among family members arises from the same source. On this basis, they investigated

obsistique fortunae, quod maximae res essent in potestate sapientis. Varietates autem iniuriasque fortunae facile veterum philosophorum praeceptis instituta vita superabat.

[18] Principiis autem a natura datis amplitudines quaedam bonorum excitabantur, partim profectae a contemplatione rerum occultiorum, quod erat insitus menti cognitionis amor, e quo etiam rationis explicandae disserendique cupiditas consequebatur; quodque hoc solum animal natum est pudoris ac verecundiae particeps appetensque convictum hominum ac societatem animadvertensque in omnibus rebus quas ageret aut diceret ut ne quid ab eo fieret nisi honeste ac decore, his initiis et, ut ante dixi, seminibus a natura datis

the origin and development of all virtues. Greatness of spirit, too, comes from the same source, which makes it easy to fight against fortune and to resist it, since the most important things are in the power of the wise person. A life lived according to the precepts of those philosophers of old easily overcomes the vicissitudes and iniquities of fortune.

[18] From these natural principles arise a variety of further goods. Some of them pertain to the contemplation of the secrets of nature: the mind has an inborn love of learning, which leads to a desire for rational explanation and argument. Furthermore, humans are the only animals with a sense of shame and decorum, eager to share the society of other humans, and intent in everything they say and do not to commit anything that is immoral or inappropriate. From these naturally given origins and—as I called

temperantia modestia iustitia et omnis honestas perfecte absoluta est.

[19] Habes, inquam, Cato, formam eorum, de quibus loquor, philosophorum. Qua exposita scire cupio quae causa sit cur Zeno ab hac antiqua constitutione desciverit, quidnam horum ab eo non sit probatum: quodne omnem naturam conservatricem sui dixerint, an quod omne animal ipsum sibi commendatum ut se salvum in suo genere incolumeque vellet, an quod, cum omnium artium finis is esset quem natura maxime quaereret, idem statui debere de totius arte vitae, an quod, cum ex animo constaremus et corpore, et haec ipsa et eorum virtutes per se esse sumendas. An vero displicuit ea quae tributa est animi virtutibus tanta praestantia? An quae de prudentia, de cognitione rerum, de coniunctione generis humani, quaeque ab eisdem de temperantia, de modestia, de magnitudine animi, de omni honestate

them earlier—seeds grow perfect temperance, moderation, justice, and all morality.

[19] This, Cato, is, in a nutshell, the philosophy of the men I'm talking about. Having laid it out, I want to know why Zeno defected from this old system, what he didn't like about it. Is it that they said that all of nature wants to preserve itself? Or that every animal is so attached to itself that it wants to maintain itself safely within its kind? Or that, since every art aims at a goal set by nature, the same must be true of the very art of life? Or that, since we consist of body and mind, we should cherish both of them, and their virtues, in and of themselves? Or did he perhaps not like the fact that the virtues of the mind are given such prominence? Or was it what was said about prudence, knowledge and learning, the interconnectedness of the human race, and about temperance, moderation, greatness of spirit, and

dicuntur? Fatebuntur Stoici haec omnia dicta esse praeclare, neque eam causam Zenoni desciscendi fuisse.

[20] Alia quaedam dicent, credo, magna antiquorum esse peccata, quae ille veri investigandi cupidus nullo modo ferre potuerit. Quid enim perversius, quid intolerabilius, quid stultius quam bonam valetudinem, quam dolorum omnium vacuitatem, quam integritatem oculorum reliquorumque sensuum ponere in bonis potius quam dicerent nihil omnino inter eas res iisque contrarias interesse? Ea enim omnia quae illi bona dicerent praeposita esse, non bona; itemque illa quae in corpore excellerent stulte antiquos dixisse per se esse expetenda; sumenda potius quam expetenda. Ea denique omni vita quae in una virtute consisteret illam vitam quae etiam ceteris rebus quae essent secundum naturam abundaret magis expetendam non esse, sed magis sumendam. Cumque ipsa virtus

morality in general? The Stoics will admit that all those things are well put, and that they aren't the reason for Zeno's defection.

[20] They'll say that those old philosophers made other significant errors, which Zeno, that eager searcher for the truth, simply could not tolerate. For what could be more perverse, more unbearable, more idiotic than to claim that good health, freedom from all pain, and unimpaired eyesight and other senses are goods—rather than to say that there is absolutely no difference between them and their opposites? For all things that those earlier philosophers called goods are really "preferred," not "good." Likewise, they made the stupid mistake of saying that the well-being of the body is to be pursued for its own sake: it's to be "chosen," not "pursued." Similarly, a life of virtue that also abounds in all the other things that are according to nature isn't

efficiat ita beatam vitam ut beatior esse non possit, tamen quaedam deesse sapientibus tum cum sint beatissimi; itaque eos id agere ut a se dolores morbos debilitates repellant.

[21] O magnam vim ingenii causamque iustam cur nova existeret disciplina! Perge porro. Sequuntur enim ea quae tu scientissime complexus es, omnium insipientiam, iniustitiam, alia vitia similia esse, omniaque peccata esse paria, eosque qui natura doctrinaque longe ad virtutem processissent, nisi eam plane consecuti essent, summe esse miseros, neque inter eorum vitam et improbissimorum quicquam omnino interesse, ut Plato, tantus ille vir, si sapiens non fuerit, nihil melius quam quivis improbissimus nec beatius vixerit.

more worthy of being pursued than a life that consists only of virtue: it's to be "chosen," not "pursued." Since virtue alone makes life so happy that it can't get any happier, wise people may be lacking certain things, even though they're perfectly happy; they will therefore make an effort to ward off pain, illness, and debility.

[21] What a great genius and what a good reason to found a new philosophy! Let's continue. What comes next is what you have explained so cleverly—namely, that all ignorance, injustice, and other vices are the same, and that all shortcomings are equal.[4] People who by disposition and study have made good progress toward virtue, but haven't quite achieved it, are supremely unhappy, and there is no difference whatsoever between their lives and those of the greatest villains. Thus Plato, that great man, unless he was

Haec videlicet est correctio philosophiae veteris et emendatio quae omnino aditum habere nullum potest in urbem, in forum, in curiam. Quis enim ferre posset ita loquentem eum qui se auctorem vitae graviter et sapienter agendae profiteretur, cumque idem sentiret quod omnes, quibus rebus eandem vim tribueret alia nomina inponentem, verba modo mutantem, de opinionibus nihil detrahentem? [22] Patronusne causae in epilogo pro reo dicens negaret esse malum exilium, publicationem bonorum? Haec reicienda esse, non fugienda? Nec misericordem iudicem esse oportere? In contione autem si loqueretur, si Hannibal ad portas venisset murumque iaculo traiecisset, negaret esse in malis capi venire interfici patriam amittere? An senatus, cum triumphum Africano decerneret, "quod eius virtute"

a sage, lived no better or more happily than any scoundrel.

This new and improved version of an old philosophy isn't going to play well in the city, forum, or senate house. Who is going to listen to the speech of someone who claims to be counseling an honorable and wise way of life and, while he really has the same views as all other people, uses new terms for the exact same things, changing only the words but keeping the substance intact? [22] Is a lawyer going to sum up his defense speech by saying that exile or the confiscation of property aren't bad things? That one should "avoid" but not "reject" them? Or that the judge shouldn't show mercy? Or if someone were giving a public speech at the moment when Hannibal is at the gates and hurling his spear over the wall, would he maintain that it's not a bad thing to be taken captive, be sold

aut "felicitate" posset dicere, si neque virtus in ullo nisi in sapiente nec felicitas vere dici potest?

Quae est igitur ista philosophia quae communi more in foro loquitur, in libellis suo? Praesertim cum, quod illi suis verbis significent, in eo nihil novetur, eaedem res maneant alio modo. [23] Quid enim interest, divitias, opes, valitudinem bona dicas anne praeposita, cum ille qui ista bona dicit nihilo plus iis tribuat quam tu, qui eadem illa praeposita nominas?
(. . .)

into slavery, be killed, or lose one's homeland? Or could the senate, when decreeing a triumph for Scipio Africanus, still use the formula "on account of his virtue and good fortune," if neither virtue nor good fortune can be truthfully ascribed to anyone except the wise?[5]

So what kind of philosophy is this, which speaks one language in public and another one in its books? Especially given that there is nothing new in the content for which they have their own words, and the facts remain the same and are just dressed up differently? [23] For what difference does it make whether you call wealth, power, and health "good" or "preferred," if the person who calls them "good" doesn't attribute any more value to them than you, who calls them "preferred"?

(. . .)

[25] Sed primum positum sit nosmet ipsos commendatos esse nobis primamque ex natura hanc habere appetitionem ut conservemus nosmet ipsos. Hoc convenit; sequitur illud ut animadvertamus qui simus ipsi, ut nos quales oportet esse servemus. Sumus igitur homines. Ex animo constamus et corpore, quae sunt cuiusdam modi, nosque oportet, ut prima appetitio naturalis postulat, haec diligere constituereque ex his finem illum summi boni atque ultimi. Quem, si prima vera sunt, ita constitui necesse est: earum rerum quae sint secundum naturam quam plurima et quam maxima adipisci. [26] Hunc igitur finem illi tenuerunt, quodque ego pluribus verbis, illi brevius secundum naturam vivere, hoc iis bonorum videbatur extremum.

[25] So let's first posit that we are attached to ourselves and have this primary natural impulse to preserve ourselves. This we agree on. Now we have to pay attention to who we ourselves are, so that we can preserve ourselves in the shape and form in which we are supposed to exist. We are human beings. We consist of mind and body, which are of a certain kind, and we need to cherish them, as this primary natural impulse tells us, and to use them as the basis for determining that greatest and ultimate good. And if what we have said so far is true, this good by necessity consists in acquiring as many as possible of those things that are according to nature, as well as the very best ones. [26] That's what those earlier philosophers thought about the greatest good. I've described it in ever so many words, but they simply called it "living according to nature."

Age nunc isti doceant, vel tu potius (quis enim ista melius?), quonam modo ab isdem principiis profecti efficiatis ut honeste vivere (id est enim vel e virtute vel naturae congruenter vivere) summum bonum sit, et quonam modo aut quo loco corpus subito deserueritis omniaque ea quae, secundum naturam cum sint, absint a nostra potestate, ipsum denique officium. Quaero igitur quomodo hae tantae commendationes a natura profectae subito a sapientia relictae sint.

[27] Quodsi non hominis summum bonum quaereremus sed cuiusdam animantis, is autem esset nihil nisi animus (liceat enim fingere aliquid eiusmodi, quo verum facilius reperiamus), tamen illi animo non esset hic vester finis. Desideraret enim valitudinem, vacuitatem doloris, appeteret

So please, let the Stoics now explain the following—or you do it: for who could do it better? Starting from these same premises, how do you arrive at the conclusion that the greatest good is "living morally" (defined as either living with virtue or living in agreement with nature)? And how and where did you suddenly leave behind the body and all those things that, while they're according to nature, are outside our control, including even appropriate action itself? I ask you: why did your wisdom suddenly jettison all those important precepts that come from nature itself?

[27] If we were looking for the greatest good, not for a human being but for a creature that consists only of a mind (let's use a made-up scenario to assist us in finding the truth), even to this pure mind your greatest good wouldn't apply. The creature would still desire health and

etiam conservationem sui earumque rerum custodiam, finemque sibi constitueret secundum naturam vivere. Quod est, ut dixi, habere ea quae secundum naturam sint, vel omnia vel plurima et maxima. [28] Cuiuscumque enim modi animal constitueris, necesse est, etiamsi id sine corpore sit, ut fingimus, tamen esse in animo quaedam similia eorum, quae sunt in corpore, ut nullo modo, nisi ut exposui, constitui possit finis bonorum.

Chrysippus autem exponens differentias animantium ait alias earum corpore excellere, alias autem animo, nonnullas valere utraque re; deinde disputat quod cuiusque generis animantium statui deceat extremum. Cum autem hominem in eo genere posuisset ut ei tribueret animi excellentiam, summum bonum id constituit, non ut excelleret

freedom from pain, would seek the preservation of itself and secure possession of the properties just mentioned, and would decide that its goal is to live according to nature. And that means, as I've said, to possess those things that are according to nature, all or most or the best of them. [28] Whatever kind of creature you invent, even if it doesn't have a body, as in our scenario, there are still in its mind properties that are similar to those in the body. And therefore, the greatest good can be none other than the one I have described.

But Chrysippus,[6] in explaining the distinctions among living creatures, says that some are outstanding in body, others in mind, and a few excel in terms of both. He then discusses what the greatest good should be for each type. But after putting humans in the category with an outstanding mind, he comes up with a greatest

animus sed ut nihil esse praeter animum videretur. Uno autem modo in virtute sola summum bonum recte poneretur, si quod esset animal quod totum ex mente constaret, id ipsum tamen sic ut ea mens nihil haberet in se quod esset secundum naturam, ut valitudo est. [29] Sed id ne cogitari quidem potest quale sit, ut non repugnet ipsum sibi.

Sin dicit obscurari quaedam nec apparere quia valde parva sint, nos quoque concedimus; quod dicit Epicurus etiam de voluptate, quae minime sint voluptates, eas obscurari saepe et obrui. Sed non sunt in eo genere tantae commoditates corporis tamque productae temporibus tamque multae. Itaque in quibus propter eorum exiguitatem obscuratio consequitur saepe accidit ut nihil interesse nostra fateamur sint illa necne sint, ut in

good for them that isn't just about the excellence of the mind, but that makes it look as though humans were nothing but a mind. There could be only one circumstance in which the greatest good could rightly be said to consist in virtue alone: if there were a creature that were all mind, but in such a way that that mind didn't have any properties that are according to nature, such as health. [29] But one cannot even imagine such a thing without running into contradictions.

If Chrysippus now says that certain things are eclipsed and disappear because they're very small, I do agree with that. Epicurus says the same about pleasure, that the smallest pleasures are often eclipsed and crowded out. But the assets of the body, which are so great, long-lasting, and many, do not fall into this category. With those things that are eclipsed because of their smallness, we can often say that it makes no

sole, quod a te dicebatur, lucernam adhibere nihil interest aut teruncium adicere Croesi pecuniae.

[30] Quibus autem in rebus tanta obscuratio non fit, fieri tamen potest ut id ipsum, quod interest, non sit magnum. Ut ei qui iucunde vixerit annos decem, si aeque vita iucunda menstrua addatur, quia momentum aliquod habeat ad iucundum accessio, bonum sit; si autem id non concedatur, non continuo vita beata tollitur.

Bona autem corporis huic sunt quod posterius posui similiora. Habent enim accessionem dignam in qua elaboretur, ut mihi in hoc Stoici iocari videantur interdum, cum ita dicant, si ad illam vitam quae cum virtute degatur ampulla aut strigilis accedat, sumpturum sapientem eam vitam potius

difference to us whether we have them or not, just as lighting a lamp in sunshine, as you said, or adding a penny to the riches of Croesus makes no difference whatsoever.

[30] Even with things that aren't eclipsed in this way, the difference they make is often not great. Say someone has lived pleasantly for ten years, and another equally pleasant month of life is added to this; that counts as a good because the additional delight makes a certain difference. But if there is no such addition, this doesn't mean that the person's life hasn't been happy.

The bodily goods are similar to this last example: they add something worth striving for. In this context, the Stoics sometimes seem to me to be joking, as when they say that if in addition to a life lived with virtue, someone had the chance of acquiring an oil flask and scraper, the wise

quo haec adiecta sint nec beatiorem tamen ob eam causam fore.

[31] Hoc simile tandem est? Non risu potius quam oratione eiciendum? Ampulla enim sit necne sit, quis non iure optimo irrideatur si laboret? At vero pravitate membrorum et cruciatu dolorum si quis quem levet, magnam ineat gratiam.

Nec si ille sapiens ad tortoris eculeum a tyranno ire cogatur, similem habeat vultum et si ampullam perdidisset, sed ut magnum et difficile certamen iniens, cum sibi cum capitali adversario, dolore, depugnandum videret, excitaret omnes rationes fortitudinis ac patientiae quarum praesidio iniret illud difficile, ut dixi, magnumque proelium. Deinde non quaerimus quid obscuretur aut intereat quia sit admodum parvum, sed quid tale sit ut expleat summam. Una voluptas e multis

person would choose the life with this addition—but it would not therefore be a happier life.[7]

[31] Is that really comparable? Shouldn't it be laughed out of court rather than deemed worthy of a reply? Wouldn't we rightly make fun of anyone who strives to acquire an oil flask? But if someone were able to free someone else from disfigured limbs or excruciating pain, that person would earn a lot of gratitude.

If that wise man were forced by a tyrant onto the torturer's rack, he wouldn't have the same expression as if he had lost his oil flask. No: he would look like someone who enters a great and difficult fight, seeing that he would have to do battle with a capital enemy—that is, pain; and he would summon all the precepts of endurance and fortitude, in order to enter this great and difficult battle, as I have called it, under their protection. Anyway, the question is not what is

obscuratur in illa vita voluptaria, sed tamen ea, quamvis parva sit, pars est eius vitae, quae posita est in voluptate. Nummus in Croesi divitiis obscuratur, pars est tamen divitiarum. Quare obscurentur etiam haec quae secundum naturam esse dicimus in vita beata; sint modo partes vitae beatae. (. . .)

[37] Vos autem, Cato, quia virtus, ut omnes fatemur, altissimum locum in homine et maxime excellentem tenet, et quod eos qui sapientes sunt absolutos et perfectos putamus, aciem animorum nostrorum virtutis splendore praestringitis. In omni enim animante est summum aliquid atque optimum, ut in equis, in canibus, quibus tamen et dolore vacare opus est et valere; sic igitur in

so small as to be eclipsed or lost, but what is able to add something to the total. In a life of hedonism, one pleasure among many ends up being eclipsed—but however small it is, it is still part of that life, which is based on pleasure. One penny is eclipsed among the riches of Croesus, but it's still part of those riches. So fine: in the happy life, those things that we say are according to nature are eclipsed. But they're still part of the happy life.

(. . .)

[37] Because all are agreed that in human life virtue holds the highest and most elevated position, and because we believe that the wise are perfect in all regards, you Stoics, Cato, dazzle our mental vision with the splendor of virtue. In every living creature, there is something that is their very best quality, as in horses or in dogs; but they still need to be free from pain and

homine perfectio ista in eo potissimum quod est optimum, id est in virtute, laudatur. Itaque mihi non satis videmini considerare quod iter sit naturae quaeque progressio. Non enim, quod facit in frugibus, ut, cum ad spicam perduxerit ab herba, relinquat et pro nihilo habeat herbam, idem facit in homine, cum eum ad rationis habitum perduxit. Semper enim ita adsumit aliquid ut ea quae prima dederit non deserat. [38] Itaque sensibus rationem adiunxit et ratione effecta sensus non reliquit.

Ut si cultura vitium, cuius hoc munus est ut efficiat ut vitis cum partibus suis omnibus quam optime se habeat—sed sic intellegamus (licet enim, ut vos quoque soletis, fingere aliquid docendi causa)—si igitur illa cultura vitium in vite

healthy. Similarly, when we praise perfect human beings, we concentrate mostly on what is their very best quality—that is, their virtue. But there you don't seem to me to be paying attention to the process of development in nature. In the case of crops, when nature has developed an ear out of a blade, it discards the blade, which is no longer important. But with human beings, when nature develops their use of reason, it doesn't do the same thing. It always adds something, but doesn't abandon its earlier gifts. [38] Thus it gives us reason in addition to sense perception, but doesn't throw out sense perception once reason has developed.

Take viticulture, whose purpose is to make the vine flourish to the greatest extent in all its parts. Let's say (because we may invent a scenario for illustrative purposes, as you Stoics also like to do) that the vine herself is put in charge

insit ipsa, cetera, credo, velit quae ad colendam vitem attinebunt, sicut antea, se autem omnibus vitis partibus praeferat statuatque nihil esse melius in vite quam se. similiter sensus, cum accessit ad naturam, tuetur illam quidem sed etiam se tuetur; cum autem assumpta ratio est, tanto in dominatu locatur ut omnia illa prima naturae huius tutelae subiciantur.

[39] Itaque non discedit ab eorum curatione quibus praeposita vitam omnem debet gubernare, ut mirari satis istorum inconstantiam non possim. Naturalem enim appetitionem, quam vocant ὁρμήν, itemque officium, ipsam etiam virtutem volunt esse earum rerum quae secundum naturam sunt. Cum autem ad summum bonum volunt pervenire, transiliunt omnia et duo nobis opera pro

of viticulture. I think she would want all the things that contribute to her growth, just as before, but she would also think that she is superior to all her parts and would decide that within the vine, there is nothing better than herself. Thus sense perception, once it is added to an organism, preserves not only that organism but also itself. And when reason comes in, it assumes such a dominant position that all those earlier natural properties are placed in its care.

[39] So reason has been put in charge of directing the lives of those inferior properties and doesn't cease to take care of them. I therefore cannot marvel enough at the self-contradictions of the Stoics. They say that natural desire (what they call *hormē*), appropriate action, and virtue all aim at those things that are according to nature. But when the Stoics come to the greatest

uno relinquunt, ut alia sumamus, alia expetamus, potius quam uno fine utrumque concluderent.

[40] At enim iam dicitis virtutem non posse constitui si ea quae extra virtutem sint ad beate vivendum pertineant. Quod totum contra est. Introduci enim virtus nullo modo potest, nisi omnia quae leget quaeque reiciet unam referentur ad summam. Nam si ea omnino neglegemus, in Aristonea vitia incidemus et peccata obliviscemurque quae virtuti ipsi principia dederimus. Sin ea non neglegemus neque tamen ad finem summi boni referemus, non multum ab Erilli levitate aberrabimus; duarum enim vitarum nobis erunt instituta capienda. Facit enim ille duo seiuncta ultima bonorum, quae ut essent vera, coniungi debuerunt; nunc ita separantur ut disiuncta sint, quo nihil potest esse perversius.

good, they leave all this behind and give us two tasks instead of one—we should "select" some things but "seek out" others—rather than making both part of the greatest good.

[40] Now you're going to say that virtue cannot be established if things other than virtue contribute to the happy life. But it's the other way around: you can't have virtue unless the things it selects and rejects all contribute to one and the same final purpose. If we don't have such things, we fall into the serious error of Aristo, forgetting the principles that we have laid down for virtue itself. However, if we do have such things, but say that they don't contribute to the greatest good as such, then we aren't far from the frivolity of Erillus and will have to come up with guidelines for two different styles of life.[8] For he says that there are two separate greatest goods—in which case they

[41] Itaque contra est ac dicitis; nam constitui virtus nullo modo potest nisi ea quae sunt prima naturae ut ad summam pertinentia tenebit.

should be combined! There is nothing more absurd than divorcing and separating them like this.

[41] Therefore the opposite of what you say is true. Virtue can in no way be established unless it pursues the first things according to nature as themselves contributing to the final and greatest good.

NOTES

Book 1. The Allure of Epicureanism

1 The conversation of Books 1 and 2 takes places in 50 BCE at Cicero's villa in Cumae. Cicero's main interlocutor is Lucius Manlius Torquatus, a young nobleman who espouses Epicureanism; Torquatus's friend Gaius Triarius is mostly a silent bystander.

2 Chrysippus (ca. 280–207 BCE) was the third head of the Stoic school and as such opposed to Epicureanism. The Kerameikos is an area of Athens, where many funerary statues were erected.

3 The Cyrenaics were a hedonistic philosophical school that held, by contrast to the Epicureans, that only pleasures based on sense perception in the present are worth pursuing. Freedom from pain would not have been considered a good (or a pleasure) by the Cyrenaics.

4 Virtue (moral excellence) was regarded as a good by many philosophical schools, most prominently the Stoics, who considered it the greatest (and, in fact, only) good (see Books 3 and 4). Traditionally, virtue could be divided into individual virtues, prominently the so-called cardinal virtues: prudence, moderation, courage, and justice. For the Epicureans, the virtues are not goods in themselves, but instrumental in procuring pleasure. In what follows, Torquatus goes through the cardinal virtues (replacing prudence with the similar wisdom) and shows how they all aim at the acquisition of pleasure.

5 That is, nonexistent. Just as we did not exist before birth, we will not exist after death, which is therefore not to be feared.

6 During his consulship in 63 BCE, Cicero uncovered a conspiracy led by the nobleman Lucius Sergius Catilina.

7 At the beginning of the conversation (1.25, not included in this selection), Cicero had maintained that some contemporary Epicureans mistakenly believe that there are mental pleasures that do not de-

rive from pleasures of the body; Torquatus here agrees that such a view is unorthodox.

8 It was a commonplace that only very few true pairs of friends had ever existed; the mythological Theseus/Peirithous and Orestes/Pylades were the prime examples.

9 The existence of three different Epicurean approaches to friendship is not attested outside *On the Greatest Good and Evil.* Cicero may be describing recent trends within Epicureanism; the first view described is probably closest to Epicurus's own. The crucial question is to what extent Epicureans can feel true affection and concern for their friends, given that, for them, friendship ultimately is but a means for procuring pleasure.

10 See 1.42–54.

Book 2. The Problems with Pleasure

1 Cicero cites a Latin legal formula (*ea res agetur*, "this will be the matter at hand"), used in Roman civil cases to define exactly what is at issue. I have

replaced this with a Latin phrase used to identify subject matter today.

2 Plato, *Phaedrus* 237b–c.

3 Metrodorus of Lampsacus (ca. 331–278 BCE) was one of Epicurus's students and a significant Epicurean philosopher in his own right.

4 The Seven Sages were wise men of Archaic Greece, about whom numerous anecdotes circulated.

5 Hieronymus of Rhodes (ca. 290–230 BCE) was a philosopher who defined the greatest good as freedom from pain.

6 According to tradition, the Roman statesman Lucius Quinctius Cincinnatus in 458 BCE was fetched from his farm to assume the emergency position of dictator.

7 Trabea and Caecilius were both writers of Roman comedy from the second century BCE.

8 The Stoics believe that any excessive emotion, even a positive one like pleasure, is a vice since it is based on a false belief: we think that the things in which we take pleasure are goods, but for the Stoics, the only good is virtue. See further Books 3 and 4.

9 The second quotation is once more from Caecilius (see Book 2, n. 7); the source of the first is unknown but must also be a comedy.

10 Heraclitus (around 500 BCE) was a Presocratic philosopher notorious for his obscure style. Plato's *Timaeus* treats cosmogony and cosmology.

11 The "first things according to nature" (*prima naturalia*) are those things that human beings are naturally predisposed to seek out. What exactly those are, and how they relate to the greatest good, is a central question of *On the Greatest Good and Evil.*

12 Another legal formula (see Book 2, n. 1).

13 The Academic Skeptic Carneades (124/3–129/8 BCE) was in the habit of discussing philosophical schools according to their views of the greatest good; his taxonomy of philosophical systems was an important source for Cicero in *On the Greatest Good and Evil.* As a Skeptic, Carneades did not himself espouse any particular view, but for the sake of argument took the position that the greatest good consists in securing the first things according to nature (2.35, not included in this selection).

14 Cicero has now rejected the Epicurean view: pleasure or freedom from pain cannot be the greatest good, which in his opinion must include the morally good. The question now remains whether moral virtue alone constitutes the greatest good (the Stoic opinion) or whether we also need external goods, crucially the "first things according to nature" (the Peripatetic opinion). This debate will be the topic of Books 3 and 4.

15 A harbor town north of Naples (modern Pozzuoli), significant for Rome's grain import.

16 A reference to Pylades, the friend of Orestes (see Book 1, n. 8).

Book 3. The Virtues of Stoicism

1 Marcus Iunius Brutus (85–42 BCE), who in the year after the publication of *On the Greatest Good and Evil* would lead the conspiracy to assassinate Julius Caesar. He had philosophical interests and wrote philosophical works himself.

2 The conversation of Books 3 and 4 takes place in 52 BCE in the library of Lucullus at Tusculum between Cicero and Marcus Porcius Cato the Younger (95–46 BCE). Cato was famous not only for his Stoicism, but also for his political and military resistance to Julius Caesar, and his suicide once he had been defeated.

3 *Appropriate* actions (Lat. *officia*, Gk. *kathēkonta*) are aimed at achieving the first things according to nature (see Book 2, n. 11), but true morality or virtue consists in the understanding and embracing of the ethical principles underlying such action. Thus, appropriate actions can be executed by the nonwise and nonvirtuous as well, but become *moral* or *correct* actions (Lat. *honestae* or *rectae actiones*, Gk. *katorthōmata*) only if executed by the wise and virtuous—that is, those with the proper understanding and attitude. Note that while externally these actions may appear to be identical, they are crucially based on different mindsets.

4 Moral action aims at the first things according to nature, as the spear is aimed at the target. However,

just as the skill of the spear thrower consists in aiming his missile well, the greatest good consists in the moral action itself, whereas the actual attainment of what was aimed for (the hitting of the target)—though certainly preferable—is not itself a "good." This ensures that humans are capable of achieving the greatest good: it is up to them to act in a moral fashion, while the success of their actions may be subject to circumstances beyond their control. Thus even the best spear thrower may not hit the target (for example, because of wind), but this does not detract from his excellence as an athlete.

5 See Book 2, n. 13. The Peripatetics are the followers of Aristotle, who held that a combination of virtue and bodily/external goods (see the following note) makes for the happiest life, by contrast to the Stoics, who believe that virtue alone is sufficient. The controversy over whether the Stoics and the Peripatetics disagree over substance or just terminology concerns whether bodily/external goods constitute actual "goods" (the Peripatetic view) or are only "preferred indifferents" (the Stoic view).

6 Bodily goods include, for example, health and unimpaired sense perception, while, for example, wealth and success are external goods. These goods are either identical, or overlap, with the first things according to nature (see Book 2, n. 11): they are things that it is natural and appropriate for human beings to pursue.

7 King Croesus of Lydia (sixth century BCE), famous for his fabulous wealth.

8 For the Stoics, only virtue is a good and only vice an evil. All other things are neither good nor bad and hence "indifferent." This doesn't mean that they are all equal: some indifferents are "preferred," others "dispreferred," and some neutral. The Stoics thus call "preferred indifferents" what other philosophers call "goods." They are to be pursued, but success or failure to acquire them does not contribute to or detract from a person's happiness, which is determined solely by their virtue, the only good there is. The early Stoic Aristo of Chios (third century) did not distinguish among indifferents, thus providing no guidance on what to pursue.

9 The Stoics were infamous for their "paradoxes," according to which only the wise person can properly be called "king" or "rich," while those ordinarily so designated fail to fulfill the necessary conditions. Tarquinius Superbus was the last of Rome's mythical kings, notorious for his tyrannical nature, which led the Romans to exile him and abolish the monarchy; Lucius Cornelius Sulla (ca. 138–78 BCE) embroiled Rome in a civil war and ruled as dictator in 81–79, causing much bloodshed among his opponents; and the wealthy Marcus Licinius Crassus (ca. 115–53 BCE), a member of the First Triumvirate with Pompey and Caesar, was killed on an ill-advised campaign in Parthia.

10 Croesus (see Book 3, n. 7), who considered himself favored by fortune, was advised by Solon, one of the Seven Sages (see Book 2, n. 4), not to believe himself happy until the last day of his life. When Croesus's kingdom was conquered by the Persian king Cyrus and Croesus himself was about to be burned to death, he recognized the wisdom of Croe-

sus's advice. From a Stoic perspective, by contrast, the wise person's happiness is perfect at any point, regardless of circumstances.

Book 4. The Limits of a Stoic Life

1 A recent law about the conduct of trials limited concluding arguments for the prosecution to two hours and for the defense to three.

2 Cicero constructs a history of philosophy according to which the successors of Plato (ca. 429–347 BCE) developed an attractive doctrine, which Zeno of Citium (335–263 BCE), the founder of Stoicism, then needlessly challenged. Speusippus (ca. 407–339 BCE) succeeded Plato as the head of his school, the Academy, and was himself succeeded by Xenocrates (d. 314 BCE) and Polemo (d. 270/69 BCE). Originally a student of Plato, Aristotle (384–322 BCE) went on to found his own school, the Lyceum or Peripatos, and was succeeded as its head by Theophrastus (ca. 370–287 BCE).

3 See 3.26.

4 As Cato explained in 3.48 (not in this selection), the Stoics hold that wisdom and virtue are all-or-nothing propositions: you are either wholly wise and virtuous, or wholly foolish and vicious, with no gradations.

5 There were two famous statesmen and generals called Scipio Africanus, but the previous mention of the Carthaginian leader Hannibal (247–183/2 BCE) points to Scipio the Elder (236–183 BCE), who defeated Hannibal in the Second Punic War.

6 See Book 1, n. 2.

7 Oil flasks and scrapers were used in the context of exercise: people rubbed themselves with oil before exercising and scraped off the dirty residue afterward.

8 For Aristo, see Book 3, n. 8. The early Stoic Erillus (third century) thought the chief good was knowledge, while also positing a subordinate good governing everyday ethics.